Searching for the

Uncommon Common Ground

THE AMERICAN ASSEMBLY was established by Dwight D. Eisenhower at Columbia University in 1950. Each year it holds at least two nonpartisan meetings that give rise to authoritative books that illuminate issues of United States policy.

An affiliate of Columbia, the Assembly is a national, educational institution incorporated in the state of New York.

The Assembly seeks to provide information, stimulate discussion, and evoke independent conclusions on matters of vital public interest.

THE AMERICAN ASSEMBLY
Columbia University

Searching for the Uncommon Common Ground:

New Dimensions on Race in America

Angela Glover Blackwell
Stewart Kwoh
Manuel Pastor

W. W. Norton & Company
New York · London

For information about permission to reproduce selections from this book,
write to Permissions, W. W. Norton & Company, Inc., 500 Fifth Avenue,
New York, NY 10110

The text and display of this book are composed in Baskerville
Composition by Molly Heron
Manufacturing by the Haddon Craftsmen Inc.
Production manager: Amanda Morrison

Library of Congress Cataloging-in-Publication Data

Blackwell, Angela Glover.
    Searching for the uncommon common ground : new dimensions on race
in America / Angela Glover Blackwell, Stewart Kwoh, and Manuel Pastor.
        p. cm. — (Uniting America)
    Includes bibliographical references and index.
    ISBN 0-393-32351-X (pbk.)
        1. United States—Race relations. 2. United States—Ethnic relations.
    3. Pluralism (Social sciences)—United States. I. Kwoh, Stewart. II. Pastor,
    Manuel. III. Title. IV. Series.

E184.A1 B5545 2002
305.8'00973—dc21

                                                                    2001055874

W. W. Norton & Company, Inc., 500 Fifth Avenue, New York, N.Y. 10110
www.wwnorton.com

W. W. Norton & Company Ltd., Castle House, 75/76 Wells Street,
London W1T 3QT

    2 3 4 5 6 7 8 9 0

Contents

Preface

The American Assembly commissioned this volume as part of its multiyear series entitled *Uniting America: Toward Common Purpose,* a project designed to help reverse some of the most difficult and divisive forces in our society. This book was initially written as a background volume for participants of the fourth Assembly in the *Uniting America* series, which focused on "Racial Equality: Public Policies for the Twenty-first Century."

Race in America continues to be a volatile, changing, and confusing issue today—just as it has throughout our history. Originally, we intended to place the Assembly on racial equality second in the *Uniting America* series, after addressing the economic inequalities that underlie so much of this topic. However, we felt additional time was warranted for developing a program on this very complex issue, and we also wanted the opportunity to learn from other efforts, including former President Clinton's Initiative for One America.

This project was based on the notion that race in America can no longer be viewed through a black-white prism, though that continues to be an important and persistent dimension. Growing numbers of Hispanics and Asian Americans—among others—and the treatment of Native Americans now and in the past all require new approaches to policy. Every day headlines shout attention to aspects of our discussions of race, e.g., Hispanics overtake blacks as the largest minority, bilingual education policies under attack, controversies over affirmative action and its substitutes, racial profiling, racial injustice, census categories, challenges to the notion of race as a valid characterization. These and other issues—some derived from our historical legacy, some a product of our dynamically changing present situation—call out for deliberations to seek common ground and avoid moving even further away from a united America. This was the terrain of our fourth Assembly in the series.

Among the specific issues addressed at the Assembly and in this volume are the following:

- In light of our rapidly changing demographics, how should we talk about race and ethnicity?
- To what extent has the country been moving toward equality of opportunity? Equality of result? How can we understand the gap between actual positive outcomes and public attitudes and perceptions?
- What is our vision of racial equality in the United States and what values underlie this vision?
- How should we decide when a universal strategy is the appropriate remedy to move toward greater equality, or when a particular one is more appropriate?
- How should the criminal justice system be reformed so as to achieve greater societal justice?
- How can we develop a fair immigration policy and a fair immigrant policy (i.e., the former focusing on people coming into the country and the other focusing on people once they are here)?
- How should we address the challenge of developing the best leaders for a multiethnic America?

The authors of this book are the three co-directors of this Assembly project: Angela Glover Blackwell, founder and president of PolicyLink; Stewart Kwoh, president and executive director of the Asian Pacific American Legal Center of Southern California; and Manuel Pastor, Jr., professor of Latin American and Latino studies and director of the Center for Justice, Tolerance and Community at the University of California at Santa Cruz. Although the authors come from diverse backgrounds and each brings unique experiences to this project, they were able to successfully implement our suggestion of creating a single essay volume rather than a series of separately written chapters. Each chapter was originally written by one of the three and subsequently cross-edited and refined by the other two. The final product, a remarkably unified piece of literature, is a testament to their abilities and dedication to this project and to racial equality and justice in general.

The *Uniting America* series began with the Assembly on economic growth and opportunity in the United States, held in June 1999 in Atlanta, and was followed by the Assembly on religion in public life, held in March 2000 at Arden House, the home of The American Assembly, in Harriman, New York. The third Assembly in the series focused on issues confronting American families and was held in Kansas City, Missouri, in September 2000. The fifth and final full Assembly in the *Uniting America* series is on enhancing collaboration among business, government, and nonprofits, held in November–December 2001 in Los Angeles. A broad goal of the overall series is to demonstrate that creative consensus building and actions, even on our most vexing problems, are both necessary and possible. To this end, these Assemblies are defining a set of policies and actions designed to help mitigate the most divisive forces in American public life. More specifically, we are providing a model for consensus building and the tools to translate this consensus into practical actions at all levels, from federal to state, local, and community.

The American Assembly developed this series in close

cooperation with a distinguished group of national leaders who form our Leadership Advisory Group and whose names are listed at the back of this volume. This group is co-chaired by three American Assembly trustees: David Gergen, JFK School of Government, Harvard University and *The NewsHour with Jim Lehrer*; Karen Elliott House, president, International, Dow Jones & Company, Inc., *The Wall Street Journal*; Donald F. McHenry, university research professor at Georgetown University's School of Foreign Service; and Paul O'Neill, former chair, ALCOA (currently on leave for government service as secretary of the treasury).

Following the final Assembly in the series, this Leadership Advisory Group will prepare and publish a short summary of the policy recommendations emanating from all five of the Assembly programs in the *Uniting America* series and launch a major initiative designed to catalyze a national dialogue around these key issues. The dialogue will include web based discussions, deliberations through a network of organizations from all sectors, community meetings, and high-level briefings.

In designing our national dialogue, we will be building upon the experience of, and precedent set by, President Eisenhower's use of the Assembly to create a national dialogue in 1960. We will compare the nature of issues analyzed in our current *Uniting America* series to those in his *President's Commission on National Goals*. This comparison will add perspective, weight, and news value to the dialogue. Building on the interest generated by this coverage, we will engage hundreds of communities throughout the United States in creating and implementing policies and actions for their communities to significantly reduce the disuniting forces that are the subject of the series.

The American Assembly gratefully acknowledges **The Ford Foundation,** the **Charles Stewart Mott Foundation,** and **The Coca-Cola Company,** whose generous support helped make this Assembly on racial equality possible.

This Assembly is part of the overall American Assembly

series, *Uniting America*. Our appreciation is also expressed
to those who have funded the series in general and other
specific Assemblies:

Major funders:
The Ford Foundation
The Goizueta Foundation
Lilly Endowment, Inc.
The Henry Luce Foundation, Inc.
Hallmark Corporate Foundation
Surdna Foundation, Inc.
The McKnight Foundation
The Coca-Cola Company
Ewing Marion Kauffman Foundation
The Rockefeller Foundation
Robert W. Woodruff Foundation

Other significant funders:
Xerox Corporation
Foundation for Child Development
Walter and Elise Haas Fund
Annie E. Casey Foundation
Bradley Currey, Jr.

Other funders:
Robert Abernethy
Genuine Parts Company
King and Spalding
Herman J. Russell Foundation
Eleanor B. Sheldon
Suntrust Banks, Inc.
Wachovia Bank
WEM

As in all our publications, the views expressed in this volume are those of its authors and do not necessarily reflect
the views of The American Assembly, nor its co-sponsors or
participants.

It is our hope and belief that the determinations of this Assembly, together with the others in the *Uniting America* series, will help to stimulate a constructive national dialogue in the United States that will contribute toward a more united America

Daniel A. Sharp
President and CEO
The American Assembly

Acknowledgments

Although the authors have worked independently and together on issues dealing with race and social justice, *Searching for the Uncommon Common Ground* would not have happened without the urging and generous support of The American Assembly. We are indebted to the Assembly and especially to Daniel Sharp for his vision and to Debra Burns Melican for her commitment and outstanding organizational efforts.

The authors collectively generated the themes, book structure, and writing tasks in a series of meetings and discussions, then took primary responsibility for specific chapters, sharing complementary research and critical commentary from each other to inform our work. Angela Glover Blackwell took the lead on chapters 2, 4, and 7; Stewart Kwoh took the lead on chapter 6; Manuel Pastor took the lead on chapters 3 and 5; and all three contributed to structuring and writing chapter 1. Pastor, with the research assistance of Javier Huizar, provided the charts, tables, and data analysis used throughout the book.

Heather Bent Tamir of PolicyLink coordinated the planning meetings and the various conference calls that enabled three very busy authors to produce this book. Her writing and her research contributions were considerable.

A book of this sort is a collaboration in the finest sense of the word. The authors could not have produced this document without the colleagues and staffs of our respective organizations, and we thank them for their extraordinary efforts. In addition to those already cited, we would like to acknowledge the writing contributions of Bonnie Tang, Julie Han, and Kathleen Chuman, who worked with the Asian Pacific American Legal Center; the writing and editing efforts of Rachel Rosner of the Center for Justice, Tolerance and Community (CJTC) at the University of California, Santa Cruz, as well as the research contributions of CJTC staff Javier Huizar, Julie Jacobs, and Andrea Del Piñal; and the editorial and writing team of Janet Dewart Bell, James Bernard, and Paulette J. Robinson of PolicyLink, along with editorial and research assistance from Katrin Sirje Kärk and Lois Roe.

Searching for the

Uncommon Common Ground

1

A Changing America*

Amerrica is undergoing dramatic demographic change. Today, just over 70 percent of Americans are white, down from well over 80 percent in 1970. African Americans have been the most numerous minority group in this country. However, Census Bureau figures released in March 2001 show that Latinos are now virtually tied in number with African Americans, portending a historic shift in

---

*As the face of America changes, so does the language to mirror those changes. People within racial groups sometimes refer to themselves as one type—"Hispanic," for example—while others (both within *and* outside the group) may prefer to call themselves "Latino." Consequently, throughout this book, the authors have deliberately chosen to use ethnic and racial terms *interchangeably*, unless a differentiation is required for specificity within a segment of that population: "Mexican Americans," "Puerto Ricans." For Americans of African descent, we interchange "African Americans" and "blacks." For those of Asian descent, we may use "Asian Americans," "Asian Pacific Americans," or "Asian Pacific Islanders." We also interchange "Native Americans" with "American Indians" and sometimes sprinkle our discussion with "America's First Peoples." Finally, we interchange "white" with "non-Hispanic white," "Anglos," and "Caucasian."

FIGURE 1-1. Changing American Demographics, 1970–2050

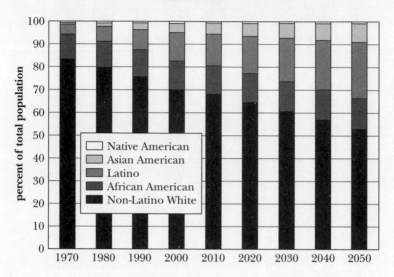

minority group dynamics. Asians are the fastest growing share of the U.S. population. It is projected that by the year 2050, the United States will be nearly a "majority-minority" country, and the Latino population will exceed all of the other minority populations combined (see Figure 1-1)—a demographic sea change.

While immigration from Latin America and Asia is primarily driving this demographic shift, the higher birth rates of Latinos and Asians, compared to white birth rates, also play a role. As Figure 1-2 shows, the minority population is much younger than the white population, indicating that the demographic trend is likely to continue, even if the United States were somehow able to stem the flow of immigrants.

What do these changes mean for America? Should race still be understood through the black-white experience—or is there an emerging ethnic mix that requires a new analytical and policy approach? Will the framework that in-

FIGURE 1-2. Projected Percentage Distribution of U.S. Resident Population by Age and Latino Origin Status for 2000

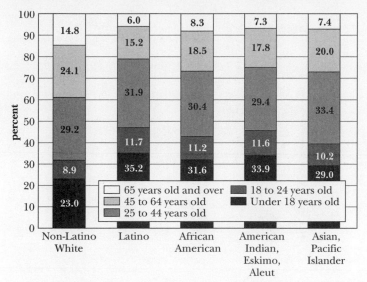

formed past thinking still be relevant to the future? Will growing American diversity inevitably lead to racial and ethnic justice?

The demographic shifts in this country that are forcing consideration of these queries are already being played out in California—often an early harbinger of the changes facing America. Figure 1-3 shows the pattern of demographic change in California from 1970 to 2000, a rough parallel of the projected changes in the U.S. population.

California has had a bumpy ride, and that may preview what is in store. In the past decade alone, the state has witnessed racially charged trials, America's most damaging instance of civil unrest in recent history, anti-immigrant political campaigns, statewide ballot measures that successfully ended affirmative action and most forms of bilingual education, black-Latino struggles over ethnic succession in political leadership, and countless other tensions.

Adding to the dynamic in California has been the mis-

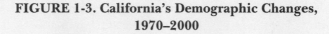

**FIGURE 1-3. California's Demographic Changes,
1970–2000**

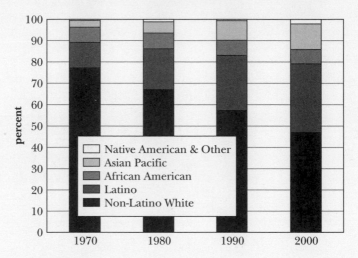

matched age profile for white Americans and people of
color. Minorities constitute a much larger share of the
young than they do the old. This fact is true at the national
level: over 25 percent of those younger than eighteen are
people of color, while nearly 85 percent of those of retirement age are white (see Figure 1-4).

In California, this racial age gap, accompanied by the
social distance between groups, has led to a reluctance of
the older and whiter population to invest in the social infrastructure needed by minority youth. As Peter Schrag notes
in *Paradise Lost: California's Experience, America's Future*
(1998), the chasm between old and young, rich and poor,
white and nonwhite has led to a fraying of the social fabric.
In particular, spending on education—on the children of
"others"—has lagged, with California dropping to the near
bottom of the states in terms of spending per pupil.

While the age and racial gaps may cause a lack of attention to the problems of young minorities, the resulting

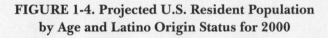

**FIGURE 1-4. Projected U.S. Resident Population
by Age and Latino Origin Status for 2000**

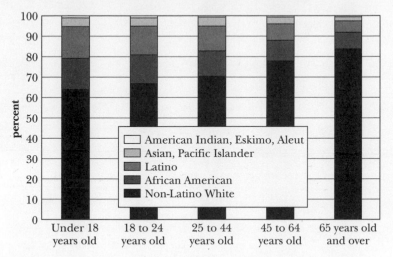

damage from inattention is not limited to them. As David
Hayes-Bautista and his colleagues argued in *Burden of Support* (1988), it is exactly these youth who will be generating
the tax revenues needed to support baby boomers in their
retirement. Restrictions on minority progress, intended or
unintended, therefore hurt more than minorities themselves, for the very future of the American economy and
society will be based on how well opportunities are opened
to all the nation's people.

Of course, not all of America is faced with these demographic changes—or at least not at the pace and scale that
have confronted California. As Figure 1-5 illustrates, the
proportion of minority populations varies significantly by
state, with some areas of the country still overwhelmingly
white.

This has sometimes led to a belief that race relations are
challenges for only the large cities and coastal and southern
states. But the challenge of becoming one America—that is,

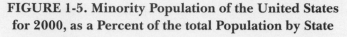

FIGURE 1-5. Minority Population of the United States for 2000, as a Percent of the total Population by State

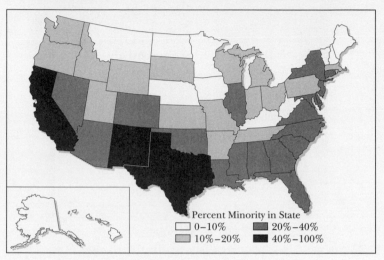

Percent Minority in State
☐ 0–10%   ■ 20%–40%
■ 10%–20% ■ 40%–100%

seeing all Americans as part of a whole—is a national one. A pure human relations approach—healing racial wounds through conversation and new understanding—will not be enough. Progress will be measured in large part by real and material gains in the areas of economic and social equality.

In *Searching for the Uncommon Common Ground*, we challenge the reader to avoid the least common denominator and aim high.

Stories of America:
How We Came to Write This Book

The authors of this volume bring diverse backgrounds and unique experiences to the consideration of these challenging issues. All three of us now live in California; issues of race and opportunity are part of the context of our lives. In our individual careers, we have sought to be agents of change. While our work ranges from scholarly pursuits to advocacy of policy, we are all committed to exploring the facts, no matter how uncomfortable they may make us or how completely they may dislodge some of our assumptions.

Writing a book about race in America, particularly given the raging debates that surround this multidimensional issue, is a daunting task. We have further complicated the task by deciding that the best approach was to include three authors, each with different perspectives and politics, and weaving together our work and world views into a single narrative. We have further challenged ourselves by focusing on the future—not what has been, but what will be.

Diverse Backgrounds, One Vision

Although the three of us are associates in other activities, we appreciate the opportunity given us by The American Assembly to write *Searching for the Uncommon Common Ground*. Working together, we have been struck by the way our personal journeys have influenced our thinking. We have decided to bring those journeys forth, so that the reader, too, can have a glimpse through our lens.

Angela Glover Blackwell. I grew up in a segregated St. Louis during the 1950s and early 1960s. From talking to my parents, reading, and interviewing people about St. Louis during those years, I know that racism there was harsh. My personal experience there as a child, however, was almost completely devoid of any awareness of racism. For I had the benefit of a web of caring adults who must have spent twenty-four hours a day figuring out ways to protect their children from racism. Part of their job was made easy by the complete separation of the races. The schools, churches, social events, service organizations, and neighborhoods where we played and volunteered were all black. But separation from whites did not satisfy these adults; their aim was higher. They wanted their children to have exposure to the best that St. Louis had to offer without coming into contact with those who would seek to diminish us. What's amazing is that they succeeded.

When I was growing up, St. Louis (then the ninth largest city in the United States) was known for its outdoor opera, its wonderful museum (with the steep hill behind used for sledding in the snow), its world-class zoo, its magnificent city park, and its symphony orchestra. While all of these attractions did not hold my interest equally, they were all a regular part of my life. These determined black adults would take us to enjoy these activities, literally shielded from the rest of the world. At the outdoor opera, for instance, the children sat on the inside seats and the adults sat on the perimeter, shooting stares and threatening gestures at any child who might embarrass them or us. When there was a special exhibit at the museum, we were taken as a group to explore the arts with our own private docent. And so it was; racism all around and the children of the black middle class in St. Louis oblivious to its sting and burn, playing in St. Louis as if it were ours.

When we weren't on reconnaissance missions, we were having a grand time within the community: Sunday school picnics, block parties, activities at the Phillis Wheatley Y (this, too, was all black), hay rides and apple picking in the fall, neighborhood Trick or Treat and Christmas caroling, social clubs, dances, and church, church, church.

Of course, it has taken the benefit of hindsight for me to appreciate the richness of the community that surrounded me as a child. At the time I felt constrained and watched. I have come to understand that for black people growing up in America during those and earlier years, community was the scaffolding around the mainstream of society that allowed us to move up. We were locked out, but we were not locked in. Through ingenuity and collaboration my black community created a parallel universe that took from the outer world what it needed to expand my horizons and make me feel that I could do anything. That strong, caring, resourceful, creative, demanding community shaped me, and its values and expectations continue to nurture me.

It was not until I went to college that I began to understand the racism that had surrounded me in St. Louis. Few of my classmates went to college because not all black children in St. Louis had the experience that I did. Our group of middle-class children, while large for a social group, represented a tiny minority of black children in St. Louis. Most of the black children were poor and were not protected. Segregation and racism hit them with full force. And those proud black adults I described were disrespected and beat down daily as they tried to earn livings, shop, buy homes, and generally provide for their families. In fact, every good thing I experienced had an ugly flip side. For example, I received a great education in St. Louis's segregated public schools partly because the well-educated, well-trained teachers that I had were not allowed to do anything else. Then, I never thought about how frustrating it must have been for the journalists, scientists, actors, singers, athletes, mathematicians, and would-be senators who taught me to spend their entire professional lives in the only careers available to them.

After college I became an organizer, a public interest lawyer, a community builder, a foundation executive, and a policy advocate. I've had many jobs, but only one project— to do something about racism, injustice, and inequality; to help build a society in which all people can thrive, contribute, and participate fully—socially and economically. In searching for solutions, I never forget that community matters.

Stewart Kwoh. I was once asked by a white waitress who was taking my restaurant order where my family was from. I answered that on my mother's side of the family, my great-grandfather was a miner in New Mexico, my grandfather was a tailor in Oakland and Stockton, CA, and that my mother was born in Stockton. The waitress interrupted me without hesitation and asked, "And how do you like your

new country?" Although both of my sons were born in Los
Angeles, I am willing to bet that they will be asked the same
question during their lifetimes. Although the stereotype of
the model minority has most recently been applied to Asian
Americans and Pacific Islanders (APIs), the most enduring
image of APIs is that of the foreigner. No matter that the
first Chinese came in large immigrant waves in the l840s to
California, U.S. society still knows very little about the API
community, although it is now over l2 million strong.

My own evolution into a civil rights advocate actually did
not begin with the concern over Asian Americans and
Pacific Islanders. It came as a result of growing up in Los
Angeles—although I was born in Nanjing, China, because
my parents were teaching there at the time—and experiencing the civil rights movement in the l960s. I was certainly influenced by my parents, who are dedicated
Christians and givers to the community. In the early l960s,
I also vividly recall the debates in my Presbyterian church.
Our minister went to march in the civil rights demonstra-
tions in the deep South and came back to a partially hostile
congregation in Los Angeles. That eye-opening experience
led to my participation in the National Conference of
Christians and Jews (NCCJ), now the National Conference
for Communities and Justice, and its brotherhood camp
(now the brotherhood and sisterhood camp). Although I
grew up in a racially integrated, moderate-income community of Echo Park and Silver Lake in Los Angeles, the
NCCJ camp widened my interracial connections and
understandings.

While I saw the Asian American and Pacific Islander student population in high school grow due to the l965
changes in the immigration laws that changed decades of
exclusion and restrictions for Asian immigrants, I did not
become familiar with racism against Asians until I attended
UCLA in l966. Becoming a student activist after a stint in
an Asian fraternity, I became part of the movement to
begin the Asian American Studies Center and later became
president of the Asian American Student Alliance. It was

only through my involvement in Asian American studies
that I began to understand the harsh racism against Asians,
including immigration exclusion and World War II concentration camps for Japanese Americans. I have been the best
man in three Japanese American weddings, and the parents of my friends never told me about their experiences in
the internment camps. Stigmatization has long kept Asian
Americans from looking at their own histories. My student
organization helped to set up community service programs
in communities like Chinatown and later organized demon-
strations against the war in Vietnam and Cambodia.

The rest is history. I had to explain to my parents that
instead of going to medical school, I was going to law
school because I was so influenced by helping to bail out
some of my fellow students who were accused of throwing
rocks at the police as they invaded the UCLA campus after
an antiwar protest. I had to explain that I decided not to
participate in law review because I needed to help an
undocumented Buddhist monk who had come to a legal
service program that I had established. I had to explain
that I rejected a number of job offers after law school
because I volunteered to start a law collective that paid
$500 per month salary.

In my work on civil rights cases dealing with Asian
Americans, African Americans, and Latinos, it is always the
valiant struggles of individuals and communities that continue to inspire me. In 1983, just as the Asian Pacific American Legal Center was established, I heard about the tragic
killing of Vincent Chin in Detroit. Actually Vincent, who
was celebrating his upcoming marriage, was killed in 1982
by two white autoworkers in what I believe was a racially
motivated killing. In 1983 his two killers received sentences
of probation and $3,000 fines for manslaughter. This case
galvanized the Asian American community and many others. I met the family and supporters of Vincent and got
involved in a campaign for federal civil rights charges to be
filed against the two killers. Vincent would be the first
Asian American to be covered by the civil rights law that

authorized such federal charges. But it was his mother, Lilly Chin, who truly inspired me. After the sentence, she decided that she needed to speak out to get support for a more just sentence against the killers. I remember she came to Los Angeles and, in a crowded Chinatown restaurant, she asked the crowd to help get justice for her son. Then she fainted. A few of us helped to revive her. Later that evening during her stay at my home, I asked her if she was okay. She said, "Stewart, there's nothing I can do to bring back Vincent, but I don't want any other mother to go through what I've been going through." While there eventually was a federal prosecution and a conviction in the first trial, an appellate reversal led to a second trial and acquittals. Mrs. Chin, whose husband died six months before Vincent was killed, decided to leave the United States and return to China, where she lives today.

It was that experience and the failures of our justice system that have led me to provide leadership to build the Asian Pacific American Legal Center into the largest API legal organization in the United States today, and to co-found the National Asian Pacific American Legal Consortium, the first pan-Asian civil rights legal organization in the history of this nation.

Manuel Pastor. Like many sons of immigrants, my story began long before my birth. My dad came to the United States in the 1930s, a young man fleeing economic despair in Cuba. His documentation was, shall we say, imperfect. But World War II came and the fervor to fill the ranks of the army eventually presented him with a stark choice: be returned to the island or go fight in Europe. He asked my cousin Carlitos to flip a coin to decide. That coin traveled with him to the war; both returned safely.

My mom was born in Tampa, FL, where her mother, an immigrant cigar-roller in a sweaty factory, had been swept off her feet by my grandfather, Joaquín, a sometime singer and sometime janitor. They headed north for economic opportunity, and my mother grew up in Spanish Harlem.

The economics did not pan out, and she eventually dropped out of her first year of high school to help support a struggling family. This put her ahead of my father, who had completed only sixth grade in his homeland. They met, they married, they never quite clawed their way to the middle class. But they were hard-working, earnest, and curious about the way the world worked—and a generation later, their son became a professor in the premier public university system in the country.

It is an immigrant story, the sort Americans often celebrate by pointing to individual initiative and drive. But it is not just our story. I grew up in a racially mixed neighborhood in Southern California, our home purchase made possible by federally sponsored loans for veterans. My father—who began his American work life as a busboy, a cook, and a janitor—moved from cleaning buildings to repairing air conditioners by virtue of a community college willing to take all comers, including those lacking strong English or the usual educational credentials. Our family income soared from poor to working class because my father's union negotiated well and occasionally struck to back up its demands. With just two books in our house— one an autobiography of Sammy Davis, Jr., entitled *Yes I Can* that I probably read more times than any other American—my passage to the university relied on strong public schools, affirmative action programs, and financial aid scholarships. In my success, I stand not alone but in the shadow of my parents' history and in debt to the social policies that helped all of our hard work pay off—and I have always felt an obligation to keep those opportunities alive.

Recognizing that you don't just make it on your own has also driven me to multiethnic alliances and coalition building. This desire to bridge also stems from my own history as both an insider and an outsider. I am Cuban American, but as low-income immigrants from an earlier era, my family never fit into the conservative, anti-Castro ethos of that community. I am a survivor of the usual problems of discrimination and educational tracking, but I came of politi-

cal age in the context of a highly nationalist Chicano movement that was sometimes wary of other Latinos. I am an
oft-published university professor, but my working-class
sensibilities have caused me to pursue research and writing
that reflect the stories of those who lack voice.

Never quite fitting in can be a source of discomfort, but
it can also generate skills of translation and accommoda-
tion. Building one America, after all, requires recognition
of our new multicultural stew—a fact I remember every
Thanksgiving when my family sits down for roast turkey
and *arroz con frijoles negros*. It involves more than acceptance of the "other"; it includes the ability to negotiate one's
own contradictions, to truly listen to another person's stories and values, to respect difference but speak for the common good. I see this in the colleagues with whom I wrote
this book; I strive for it in myself.

Like Angela and Stewart, my professional life has been
devoted to social justice, sometimes through research and
teaching, sometimes through public advocacy and organizing. One view of why we do this has us doing good; the
reality is that we know little else. Living a life with purpose
has its own rewards, of course, but beyond that is a simple
truth: at the end of the day, I need to honor the struggles
of my mother and father by working to ensure that some
measure of fairness is afforded to all Americans.

As stated earlier, the three of us are now based in the cut-
ting-edge social environment of California, where we have
a chance to witness dramatic changes first-hand. As a team
we are representative of the state's multiculturalism. Having revealed our stories, we ask the reader: what brings you
to a consideration of these issues? Why and how is race
salient in your life—and why do you choose to spend valuable time considering what America needs to do to realize
its dreams of equality and opportunity?

Taking a moment to reflect on what drives us, and you,
to this topic is not inconsistent with the fact based analysis
and commitment to pragmatic policies that occupy most

of the attention in *Searching for the Uncommon Common Ground*.

The struggle for full rights for all Americans is a long one, and despite our optimism, it probably will not be resolved in our lifetimes. Maintaining energies and building momentum along the way require that we reflect on the journey and our reasons for taking it. It requires that we evoke from all of us the best in America and that all Americans join us in this exploration.

New World, New Dimensions

Traditionally, the entry point to understanding the social dynamics associated with race, discrimination, and group advancement has been through the black experience. While there are numerous instances of racial or ethnic exclusion and oppression—the taking of Native American lands; the dispossession of Mexicans in the Southwest; the exclusion of Asians from legal immigration; prejudice and restrictions against the Irish, Jews, and other white ethnics; the internment of Japanese Americans during World War II—slavery, Jim Crow, and the struggle for black empowerment have left the deepest mark on race relations.

Indeed, the dominance of the black-white paradigm is reflected even in census materials. Until the early 1970s, data were not collected separately on Latinos, and many of the available statistical series based on census tabulations are broken up into white and "black or other." (This is the case, for example, with many of the long-term series on unemployment and poverty. For a brilliant dissection of the meaning of race in the census collection process, see Rodríguez, 2000.) And while the civil rights movement proved to be empowering to a wide range of groups, it was clearly the conditions of African Americans that provoked both moral outrage and effective mobilizing for justice. America's diversity has ushered in a new era in race relations, with increased socializing and interaction across racial and ethnic groups. This new-found social ease has led some to question the continued existence of racism. Liberals and conservatives disagree about the extent to which the system or the individual is to be blamed for continuing inequity.

At issue is the larger question of racial justice. If one determines that the structure is the primary reason for continuing inequality, the politics of change are still complicated. Should organizing and policy be targeted to specific disadvantaged groups, including the mobilization of specific communities to defend their own interests? Or does this lead to further fragmentation and separation, suggesting that it may be better, as in the case with Social Security, to take a universal approach? Consider, for example, Randall Robinson's recent appeal for reparations in *The Debt: What America Owes to Blacks.* It remains to be seen if this approach will move politicians to action or if William Julius Wilson's coalitional approach, articulated in *The Bridge Over the Racial Divide: Rising Inequality and Coalition Politics,* will hold sway.

What is the relationship between a high-level gathering of elites, made comfortable in their differences by similar levels of education or stature, and the block-by-block ethnic tensions engulfing many of America's biggest cities? Will attention to diversity yield a more just society or is diversity of leadership really just skin deep? Can the country achieve racial equality with a focus just on material progress—or is a new moral vision required of the sort that animated the civil rights movement and captured the imagination of a generation across race and class?

Five Dimensions in the Debate on Race

Searching for the Uncommon Common Ground attempts to delve into the multifaceted dimensions of race that have impact on America's quest for equality. It seeks to provoke new thought and shed new light on approaches and policies needed in a new era. With that in mind, five themes are presented that frame discussions in this book.

- The black-white paradigm versus multiculturalism
- Diversity versus racial and social justice
- Universal versus particular strategies
- National versus local responsibility
- Structural factors versus individual initiative

The Black-White Paradigm versus Multiculturalism. First is the black-white paradigm versus a multicultural framework. We concur with those who suggest that a changing America, specifically the rapid growth of the Latino and Asian populations, implies that previous understandings of race may not suffice. An analysis of the 1992 Los Angeles civil unrest—perhaps the most racially charged event of the past decade—makes the point.

Provoked by outrage over the not-guilty verdict in the trial of police officers accused of beating Rodney King, an African American motorist, the three days of rioting, looting, and arson were portrayed in the national media as a largely black-driven phenomenon (Smith, 1994). In fact, Latinos were apparently the most numerous among those arrested, and the property damage actually occurred in neighborhoods that were nearly 50 percent Latino (Pastor, 1995). Poverty was a driving factor. Understanding either the pattern of unrest or strategies for alleviating poverty from a strictly black-white perspective would be incomplete in this case, since poverty in Latino communities is characterized by the working poor, while African Americans suffer from high rates of joblessness.

A pure black-white perspective would also miss the nuances of the Asian American experience. As the data presented later will make clear, many Asian American groups are doing relatively well on the economic front—the usual marker of the effects of discrimination. Does this mean that disadvantage is absent? Not if one considers the pattern of anti-Asian hate crimes, a poverty rate that is twice that of white Americans, the "racial profiling" of Asians as a foreign and distrustful "other," and the explicit example of Wen Ho Lee, the Chinese American scientist accused of transmitting nuclear secrets to enemies of the United States.

Of course, too much can be made of the new multicultural framework—the pattern of residential segregation and poverty for Latinos in the L.A. example and the stereotypic treatment of Lee and other Asian Americans have much to do with how the black-white dynamic has structured the way Americans understand and treat race. At the same time that new thinking is needed to address the implications of changing diversity, it is also essential to understand that the black-white tension remains fundamental, defining, and persistent, and it colors the experience of all minorities in this country.

Diversity versus Racial and Social Justice. When discussing the state of race relations in America, many point to the success and acceptance of African Americans as cultural icons and heroes: teenage boys of all colors look up to Michael Jordan, teenage girls admire the success of Venus Williams, and struggling parents of all races draw lessons from the calm example of Bill Cosby, splashed across our television screens in constant reruns. Examples of individual advancement abound, and the cabinet of President George W. Bush rivals that of his Democratic predecessor, Bill Clinton, in its diversity.

But diversity at the top does not necessarily spell justice at the bottom. The extraordinarily high poverty rates of blacks, Latinos, and Native Americans should be of concern to everyone. Even the "model minority" Asian community faces economic hardships, exceeding those in white America. Educational opportunities are uneven, police treatment is disparate, and concentrated poverty is especially severe among minority Americans. Achieving racial equality will require more than changing the skin tones of America's business and upper-middle classes, important as this may be. While diversity is to be supported, it must be effectively tied to improving the life chances for all Americans who have been left behind.

Universal versus Particular Strategies. Those most engaged in the pursuit of racial equality have debated the merits of adopting what are termed universal or particular strategies. Education provides fertile ground for considering the difference in approaches. Bilingual education is viewed by many Latino and Asian leaders as especially critical for a full transition to American society—but pursuing a particularist approach that meets the needs of specific groups has triggered a backlash focused on whether such an educational approach moves away from what is viewed as assimilation into the mainstream culture.

Those taking a more universal approach may instead stress the need to increase spending on all students, looking thereby to craft policies that avoid initial suspicions and unite groups around a commonly shared goal. The economic parallel is clear: minorities have generally done much better when the overall economy experiences a long-term economic boom, partly because it takes a while for recovery to reach inner-city and other minority communities. This has led some, such as William Julius Wilson, to argue that a government commitment to full employment might be the best vehicle for black advancement, especially because such growth will benefit potential allies in the white community as well. Even the key issues of the civil rights movement have been anchored in universalism—defenders of affirmative action have often noted that the main beneficiaries have been white women (and their families), suggesting that a seemingly particular and race based program (at least in the public perception) actually has broader benefits.

Certain issues, however, like the composition of America's prison population and policies toward immigrant integration, cannot be approached without a firm acknowl-

edgment of the role of race. Universalism works by not
papering over the different experiences of Americans, but
rather by pointing out how Americans are part of the same
social fabric. Underinvestment in "someone else's children"
can create problems for everyone. As with the country's
flawed urban policies, subsidized racially driven sprawl can
damage the environment, create alienation, and limit the
ability of regions to achieve economic, social, and environmental viability that benefit all.

National versus Local Responsibility. The debate here centers
on whether the federal government should play a role in
reducing racial inequality or whether progress is best left to
local jurisdictions. Long-time civil rights activists can be a
bit wary of localism—after all, the assertion of states' rights
was the cover for maintaining Jim Crow, and it required a
national movement and federal intervention to transform
the social landscape of the South. At the same time, new
neighborhood based efforts, particularly those coming
under the rubric of "community building" (Walsh, 1997;
Kretzmann and McKnight, 1993), hold great promise for
reshaping areas plagued by weakened institutions and shat-
tered economies. In this effort, many of the key actors are
local leaders and grassroots organizers—not bureaucrats
from Washington or state capitals.

But the national sets the context for the local. The
sprawl that facilitated the departure of many white Americans from our central cities was not simply a result of individual decisions or local zoning laws, although both
contributed. Equally important were federal lending
programs, including the mortgage interest deduction that
facilitated the purchase of suburban homes, nationally supported highway construction that encouraged local com-
muting, and large federal subsidies for expansion of sewer
and water infrastructure to outlying areas. On another
front, no matter what efforts local communities may make
to reduce crime, improve police protection and treatment,
and avoid the criminalization of their young, the federal

laws that mandate differential sentencing for crack versus powder cocaine ensure the same youthful mistake—involvement with drugs—will have ramifications at the community level that differ substantially by race.

This book argues for both understanding and celebrating local initiatives—and for setting the larger context for those to be successful. The federal Community Reinvestment Act, for example, requires that banks provide loans in their service areas. This requirement has facilitated individual initiative by providing the opportunities for local residents to secure loans, buy houses, and start businesses—and empowered community development corporations to expand the stock of affordable housing in lower-income areas. Even banks have recognized the importance of the act, which has broadened their customer base and diversified their marketing.

Structural Factors versus Individual Initiative. This national versus local debate parallels the discussion of structural factors versus individual initiative. Activists and liberals often tend to focus on impediments writ large: public policies that stack the decks against community advancement. Conservatives tend to stress the individual success stories: with enough of what Latinos call *ganas,* or individual desire, anyone can make it. Stories or anecdotes, however, should be illustrative of a truth and not used to obscure the facts or tell a story that is marginal to the data. After all, the rules are sometimes set in such a way that individual advancement requires Herculean efforts. Conversely, success stories are often predicated on welcoming public structures: educational systems that do their job for the poorest in America, military training that sets aside race in the name of achieving unit coherence and combat readiness, and outreach and set-aside programs that give minority small businesses their first crack at proving their worth. *Searching for the Uncommon Common Ground* celebrates the individual and recognizes that negative outcomes can be the results of personal failings or lack of initiative. At the same time, it

stresses how best to design policies that allow all Americans
to realize their potential.

A Call on Leadership

Finally, there is a seeming tension between moral leadership and pragmatic policies. Dr. Martin Luther King, Jr.'s
famous speech, the "I have a dream" oration delivered on
the steps of the Lincoln Memorial in 1963, has become fod-
der for conservatives and liberals alike. His hope that his
children would be judged on the "content of their character and not the color of their skin" has become a basis for
arguing against affirmative action—an argument that
ignores the need for public policies around expanding economic opportunity that were part and parcel of his later
work. In part because of this capacity for multiple interpre-
tations of the message, those seeking to move beyond diversity to achieve social justice have tended to focus on the
policy steps needed to get there. But an animating moral
vision is needed to tie together people and the various policies that constitute a 21st-century program for achieving
racial justice. The need for leadership development is a
central part of this story. In this regard, two points are key.
The first is understanding that America is moving into a
world where "minoritarian" leadership will be needed.
When no group is dominant, at least demographically, it is
difficult to simply assert a solution. Instead, one needs to
search for commonalities and community. Leadership is a
skill many minority leaders have been forced to develop
through years of being the first, only, and lonely participant
in "broader" discussions. They, therefore, have something
to teach. Being a minority leader hones skills that will
become increasingly critical for all Americans, particularly
as America realizes its destiny in an increasingly global
world. Second, leadership development is a long-term
process. It will require significant investments, financial
and personal, in new conversations and programs.

In the meantime, there are issues that will require imme-

diate attention from policy makers and activists. One is
reminded of the words of a community leader shortly after
the Los Angeles civil unrest: called to yet another urgent
meeting of minority representatives and looking around
the room at the people offering a frantic flurry of sugges-
tions about new programs and policies, he began to worry
that steps quickly taken might not lead to a road firmly con-
structed. As the discussion hit a lull, he leaned back and
commented: "There is an immediate need to think long
term."

In America today, there is an urgent need to think long
term. This book welcomes those of good will to engage in a
conversation about the future of America.

The Plan of the Book

Searching for the Uncommon Common Ground seeks to explore
various dimensions related to the pursuit of racial equality,
setting the stage for such a conversation with facts, insights,
and analysis. Chapter 2 begins with a deeper discussion of
the continuing problem of race in America. It acknowledges the growing racial and ethnic diversity in this country but notes that with increased diversity has come not
only increased racial acceptance but also rising inequality as
Latinos and Asians face injustices that many African Americans and Native Americans have experienced and continue
to experience. The chapter grounds understanding of
America's continuing dilemma in the black-white paradigm
that remains defining, embedded, and persistent. In a time
of increasing diversity, many are tempted to look past the
black-white dynamic. Chapter 2 shows that social and economic justice will not be achieved for American people of
color until the black-white issue is honestly and productively engaged.

Chapter 3 takes up the issue of diversity versus justice
and sets the stage for considering the problems of material progress—much has changed in the way of attitudes,
but much less has been accomplished in the realm of eco-

nomic and social advancement. Income inequality remains significant, particularly between white Americans
and African Americans and Latinos. Because wealth is
even more unequally distributed, the prospects for the
future are not good. One bright spot exists in the sharp
growth in minority business, although problems with
obtaining a fair share of credit continue to constrain many
minority entrepreneurs.

The chapter argues that discrimination and structural
barriers, such as urban isolation and social geography, play
major roles in the persistence of inequality. An additional
reason, and one linked to the concentration of poverty, is
the role of social networks that connect people of like social
stations, leading to upward trajectories for some and continuing limitations for others. All of these factors constrain the
economic and social potential of the nation by eroding the
human and social capital necessary for economic growth.

This book is not the first to consider the deeply
entrenched continuing disparities in America and the
strategies that have worked to alleviate them. Chapter 4
seeks to capture the lessons learned about what it takes to
achieve racial justice. It seeks to debunk the myth that
nothing works by lifting up themes and principles that have
proven effective, ranging from federal policies and programs to a focus on rights and community building.

Chapter 5 highlights some of the policy issues likely to
occupy the attention of activists and policy makers concerned about racial equity in the coming years and recommends solutions to them. While the focus is on "cutting
edge" issues—areas that are relatively new on the national
screen but that are expected to gain prominence—we
begin with a consideration of education, a topic of continuing importance and one on which some degree of consensus seems to be emerging. We frame this discussion and the
rest of the chapter in terms of the relative merits of universal versus particular approaches to policy making and political mobilization; we argue that while much can be gained
by focusing on common ground concerns such as educa-

tion, it is also important to insist on a discussion of tougher issues, such as inequities in the criminal justice system, that are seen as more far afield of the mainstream because of their special importance to minority populations.

We therefore consider a range of issues falling in various places along the universal-particular spectrum. While we do not pretend that our list is exhaustive, we highlight the following as key areas for new ideas and policies: the impacts of suburban sprawl and the need for regional approaches to policy making; the disparities in exposure to environmental hazards, with resulting impacts on health and economic development; the widening gap in the digital economy, partly because of differences in access to high-technology opportunities but also because the "new economy" is generating as many new jobs at the bottom of the labor market as at the top; the need to recognize the continuing flow of new immigrants and ease the integration of these communities into American life; and the disparities in the criminal justice system that make it more likely that African Americans and Latinos will be marked with records that impede their ability to integrate productively into the society and economy.

Chapter 6 considers the kind of leadership that will be needed to chart a new course for America. It argues that effective leaders of the future will be those who are good listeners, value inclusion, and take a collaborative approach to problem solving. This chapter also examines effective leadership development models.

Chapter 7 summarizes the arguments of this book and lays out the elements in the search to find, in our uncommonness, common ground that can stir Americans to action.

References

Hayes-Bautista, David, Werner O. Schink, Jorge Chapa, and Douglas X. Patino. 1988. *Burden of Support: Young Latinos in an Aging Society*. Stanford, CA: Stanford University Press.

Kretzmann, John P., and John L. McKnight. 1993. *Building Communities From the Inside Out: A Path Toward Finding and Mobilizing a Community's Assets*. Evanston, IL: Center for Urban Affairs and Policy Research, Northwestern University.

Pastor, Manuel. 1995. "Economic Inequality, Latino Poverty and the Civil Unrest in Los Angeles." *Economic Development Quarterly*, Vol. 9, No. 3.

Robinson, Randall. 2000. *The Debt: What America Owes to Blacks*. New York: Plume.

Rodríguez, Clara E. 2000. *Changing Race: Latinos, the Census, and the History of Ethnicity in the United States*. New York: New York University Press.

Schrag, Peter. 1998. *Paradise Lost: California's Experience, America's Future*. New York: New Press, distributed by W. W. Norton.

Smith, Erna. 1994. *Transmitting Race: The Los Angeles Riot in Television News*. Research Paper R-11, Joan Shorenstein Barone Center, John F. Kennedy School of Government, Harvard University.

Walsh, Joan. 1997. *Stories of Renewal: Community Building and the Future of Urban America*. New York: The Rockefeller Foundation.

Wilson, William Julius. 1999. *The Bridge Over the Racial Divide: Rising Inequality and Coalition Politics*. Berkeley, CA: University of California Press.

2

Color Lines

Race is a difficult subject for Americans. Many simply do not want to talk about it. Those who try often find the discussions unproductive, particularly with members of other races. There is an almost palpable fatigue that hangs in the air whenever the subject comes up. To the ears of many white Americans, cries of racism sound shrill. On the other hand, many black Americans are exasperated and angry that they must continue to face discrimination in their everyday lives. Latinos are often tired of hearing the issue of race reduced to black and white. Asians are increasingly boxed into a corner, monolithically considered the "model minority" by the larger society and often resented by other minorities. To Native Americans, it must appear that the atrocities committed against them have been forgotten. And, of course, there are Americans of all racial backgrounds who feel that racism no longer exists and that the term is no longer relevant.

Whether spoken or not, there is growing currency to the idea that the nation has crossed into a post-racial era. The country's growing diversity is seen as having washed away the stark images of yesterday—the blocked schoolhouse doors and the burning crosses. America's increasing diversity is considered as evidence of tolerance and, by extension, justice. The black-white paradigm is seen as the old story, while diversity is the new story.

In actuality, there is no "old" story and there is no "new" story—only one evolving story. While there have been economic and social gains among people of color in the latter part of the 20th century, inequity remains a facet of the American social order. There is a racial aspect to this inequity, rooted in the painful history of racial oppression. Certainly, at the dawn of this new era, no one can talk credibly about race without understanding diversity and recognizing that racial issues do not come in just black and white. However, to fully grasp the myriad challenges of this growing diversity, one must examine how the history between blacks and whites has unfolded and how racial prejudice and disadvantage have become embedded in U.S. institutions and society.

The genocidal assault on Native Americans set the stage in the United States for racism and the mistreatment of people of color. This act made it acceptable for Native Americans to be exterminated, uprooted from their land, and removed from the U.S. mainstream, and built racial inequities into the foundation of U.S. society. Native Americans have never recovered from their treatment at the hands of white settlers and remain one of the country's most disadvantaged groups.

Slavery and Jim Crow further cemented racial divisions in U.S. society, inflicting wounds that cut deep, creating a dynamic that has framed all interactions across race and ethnicity. Clearly, the face of diversity and inequality has changed since the beginning of the civil rights movement; the black-white paradigm, however, remains defining, embedded, and persistent. The experiences and struggles of all racial and ethnic groups, while particular, are shaped by this fact. When new Americans arrive in this country, they enter into a polarized situation that is defined and shaped by the history of racial prejudice against African

Americans and the unfair opportunity structure that has been the result. Social and economic justice for all Americans will not be achieved until the black-white dilemma is honestly and productively confronted.

This chapter explores America's increasing diversity as a way of understanding the lens through which approaches to racial justice should be viewed. It finds that an understanding of the persistent disadvantage due to race that permeates the black-white context is necessary but not sufficient for exploring the full dimensions of racial justice. America's growing diversity calls for new thinking about the structures of inequity. Asians and Latinos face challenges that African Americans do not. There are needs that would not be identified solely by employing a black-white lens. The key is to avoid losing sight of the continuing truths, while adjusting to new realities.

Growing Diversity

As discussed earlier, the demographic landscape of America is changing dramatically. The most recent Census Bureau data show that Latinos are now as numerous as African Americans and are projected to become the largest minority population by the middle of the decade. By 2003, it is expected that eighteen of the twenty-five most populous U.S. counties will have larger Latino than black populations (Davis, 2000). Furthermore, by mid-century, more than 40 percent of the population will consist of racial and ethnic minorities. Of the mainland states, California and New Mexico are forerunners of this national demographic trend, with the percentage of nonwhites in those states already outnumbering that of white Americans. Texas and Florida are close behind.

California is a microcosm of what is to come. Census Bureau estimates for 1999 showed that this state had entered a new racial frontier: its white population dipped below the 50 percent mark, ceding majority status to non-white groups. By the time of the 2000 census, Latinos were

32.4 percent of the population, up from 26 percent in 1990, while Asians represented 12.1 percent of the population, up from 9.1 in 1990. African Americans constituted 7 percent of the population, and Native Americans less than 1 percent. California's white population, meanwhile, had dropped from 57.2 percent in 1990 to 46.7 percent of the state's 33.9 million residents.

Los Angeles County's Latino and Asian populations increased significantly during the 1990s. The Latino population grew by 26.6 percent between 1990 and 2000 and represented the nation's largest Latino population, by county, numbering 4.2 million. The city of Los Angeles, meanwhile, can now claim a Salvadoran population "equal to or greater than" that of San Salvador, the capital of El Salvador (Davis, 2000). The Asian population in the county increased by 35.1 percent over the same period and also represented the nation's largest Asian population, by county, at 1.2 million. Countywide, the black population posted no growth, while white residents decreased by around 650,000.[1]

Asian American and Latino immigrants are no longer primarily gravitating to six states: California, New York, Texas, Florida, New Jersey, and Illinois. In record numbers, they are moving to states such as Nevada, Arkansas, North Carolina, Georgia, and Iowa—termed "new immigrant states" by the Urban Institute (Fix and Zimmermann, 2000)—transforming the American landscape. During the 1990s the immigrant population in these "new immigrant states" grew twice as fast as the number in traditional gateway states—California, Texas, and New York (Fix and Zimmermann, 2000). Drawn by job opportunities generated by a strong economy, they are looking for slower paced, rural lifestyles similar to those in their native lands. Nevada was the fastest growing state in the 1990s, seeing its population double. Much of that growth came from Asians and Latinos settling in Las Vegas to fill new construction and service industry jobs. Nevada's Asian population soared 123.7 percent to 88,208—the largest such increase in the nation; its Latino population outpaced even that, rising 144.6 percent, to 304,364.

The Atlanta region experienced some of the most significant increases in the Latino population. In Gwinnett County, the Latino population rose dramatically—215.6 percent—and in Cobb County, Latinos registered a growth of 158.9 percent. The Asian population also expanded dramatically, up 180.7 percent in Gwinnett County and 135.7 percent in Cobb. Jobs in construction, food processing, and textiles served as magnets.

Large numbers of Latino immigrants—often actively recruited by meat packing and poultry companies—are transforming small towns in North Carolina. In Siler City, for instance, which was demographically black and white a decade ago, Latinos now comprise 40 percent of the population, or more than 3,000 residents (Yeoman, 2000). Arkansas had the biggest percentage growth among Latinos of all states, at 170.3 percent. A Latino influx has occurred in Salt Lake City where 40 percent of elementary school children are Latino (Davis, 2000).

Not generally known for its racial diversity, Massachusetts is part of this growing phenomenon. It has over half a million foreign-born residents, close to 40 percent of whom entered between 1980 and 1990 (Fix and Passel, 1994). Lowell, a former garment manufacturing community turned high-tech job center, has a thriving Asian community and the second largest number of Cambodian Americans in the United States, behind Long Beach, CA (Fletcher, 2000).

The heartland is not immune from shifting demographic forces either. Latino immigrants, mostly of Mexican heritage, have been steadily arriving in central and western Iowa over the past decade to work in meat packing plants. In fact, Governor Tom Vilsack has openly invited immigrants to settle in the state, unveiling a bold plan to create a supportive and thriving atmosphere for them. He believes this approach is needed to help solve Iowa's labor shortage.

The growing diversity in the country is reinforced by the diversity that exists within racial and ethnic groups themselves.

The Latino community, for example, is actually many

different communities. As Figure 2-1 delineates, Mexicans comprise the bulk of U.S. Latinos, with Puerto Ricans and Cubans being the next largest of single "national" groupings.[2]

Even though they share a common heritage, their experiences in America markedly diverge. The Mexican-origin population is younger and has significant education gaps (see Tables 2-1 and 2-2).

FIGURE 2-1. Composition of U.S. Latino Population, 2000

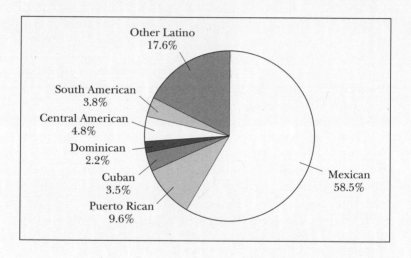

This community also has a very high rate of labor force attachment—a fact that belies the welfare-using stereotypes portrayed in anti-immigrant campaigns (see Box 2-1)—but remains low income, an outcome that suggests that the problem is less a lack of job connection than it is connection to low-wage sectors in the economy.

The Puerto Rican experience differs. There we find very high rates of female-headed households, a very high rate of detachment from the labor force, and the lowest income levels and homeownership rates of any Latino group.

TABLE 2-1. Demographic Characteristics of U.S. Latino Population, 1999

PERCENT DISTRIBUTION

CHARACTERISTIC	White	Black	Latino, total	Mexican	Puerto Rican	Cuban	Central, South	Other Latino
AGE DISTRIBUTION								
Under 5 years old	6.9	8.6	11.2	12.2	10.3	5.5	9.4	10.0
5 to 14 years old	14.2	18.8	19.4	20.6	18.5	10.7	16.7	19.9
15 to 44 years old	43.9	47.3	49.6	50.2	47.7	39.2	53.7	44.8
45 to 64 years old	22.2	17.5	14.4	12.6	16.9	26.8	15.9	17.8
65 years old and over	12.9	7.8	5.4	4.4	6.5	17.7	4.2	7.6
FAMILY TYPE								
Married couple	80.7	47.1	68.0	69.9	56.7	79.2	66.6	61.7
Female householder, no spouse present	14.2	45.1	23.7	21.3	37.2	17.0	23.7	30.6
Male householder, no spouse present	5.1	7.8	8.2	8.7	6.1	3.7	9.7	7.8
EDUCATIONAL ATTAINMENT								
Persons 25 years old and over								
High school graduate or higher	58.4	61.6	56.1	49.7	63.9	70.3	64.0	71.1
Bachelor's degree or higher	25.9	15.5	10.9	7.1	11.1	24.8	18.0	15.0

Source: Statistical Abstract of the United States 2000, Tables No. 41, 45; www.census.gov/prod/www/statistical-abstract-us.html

TABLE 2-2. Economic Characteristics of U.S. Latino Population, 1999

				PERCENT DISTRIBUTION				
CHARACTERISTIC	White	Black	Latino, total	Mexican	Puerto Rican	Cuban	Central, South	Other Latino
LABOR FORCE STATUS								
Civilian labor force	67.3	65.8	67.7	68.2	61.7	62.6	71.6	66.9
Employed	64.8	60.6	63.4	63.7	56.6	59.7	67.5	62.9
Unemployed	2.5	5.3	4.4	4.5	5.1	2.9	4.1	4.0
Not in labor force	32.7	34.2	32.3	31.8	38.3	37.4	28.4	33.2
FAMILY INCOME IN 1998								
Less than $5,000	2.0	6.5	4.8	4.5	6.8	3.6	4.3	6.6
$5,000 to $9,999	2.9	9.5	7.1	7.4	10.4	4.4	4.6	6.4
$10,000 to $14,999	4.7	9.5	10.4	10.7	10.4	11.8	9.3	
$15,000 to $24,999	11.6	17.9	18.9	20.5	15.2	14.2	18.4	13.5
$25,000 to $34,999	12.6	13.6	17.1	18.4	16.9	10.4	16.0	13.7
$35,000 to $49,999	17.1	14.7	16.1	15.8	14.8	13.0	18.1	19.0
$50,000 or more	48.9	28.4	25.6	22.8	25.6	42.6	29.4	31.2
Median income (dol.)	$49,023	$29,404	$29,608	$27,883	$28,953	$39,530	$32,676	$35,264
Families below poverty level	8.0	23.4	22.7	24.4	26.7	11.0	18.5	18.2
Persons below poverty level	10.5	26.1	25.6	27.1	30.9	13.6	18.9	23.6
HOUSING TENURE								
Owner-occupied	70.3	45.5	45.2	48.7	32.8	57.6	34.7	45.9
Renter-occupied	28.1	53.0	54.8	51.3	67.2	42.4	65.3	54.1

Source: Statistical Abstract of the United States 2000, Tables No. 41, 45; www.census.gov/prod/www/statistical-abstract-us.html

Box 2-1. Image and Immigrants

"They keep coming. . . ." This was the tag line, accompanied by images of Mexicans darting across the border, for an influential ad sprung during the 1994 reelection campaign of California Governor Pete Wilson. Keyed to accompany Proposition 187, the ballot measure designed to cut off public services to undocumented immigrants, the ad enraged Mexican American voters who felt that the ad was indirectly targeted at them and would encourage discrimination against even U.S.-born residents.

Figure for Box 2-1. Comparison of Recent Immigrant Households (Mexican and Armenian) on Public Assistance in Los Angeles County

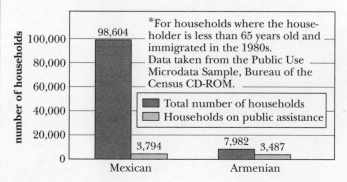

While many debated the civil rights implications of the proposition, few questioned the underlying notions prompting the campaign and the ad: that immigrants were straining the welfare state and that the majority of

those to blame were from the Golden State's neighbor to
the south.

In a telling study of Latino immigration to southern California, Manuel Pastor (2001) tried to construct a statistical profile of welfare use among different types of
immigrants. Like many other researchers, he found that
lower-income immigrants actually make little use of public assistance, primarily because of fear that this may
ensnare them into problems with the Immigration and
Naturalization Service.

Perhaps most interesting was his attempt to determine
the ethnicity of those accessing public assistance. Focusing on the largest Latino immigrant group, Mexicans,
and the largest white immigrant group, Armenians, he
calculated both the number of immigrant families and
the number using public assistance. As illustrated in the
figure, Mexicans had twelve times as many immigrant
households as did Armenians but both groups had
about the same number of households utilizing public
assistance.

Why then were Mexicans rather than Armenians the target of the ad campaign? It is true that the large Latino
immigrant population poses other fiscal costs, particularly given the heavy presence of immigrant children in
the public school system. Still, there was a startling gap
between image and reality in the consideration of immigration and immigrants, suggesting that the real reason
for such "racial profiling" was the hope that it might
appeal to voters concerned about the changing ethnic
character of the state. Instead, the Latino backlash
encouraged a mobilization of immigrants to gain citizenship, register, and vote, and this has swelled the power of
the Latinos in the California electorate.

Meanwhile, Cubans are much older, generally better educated, and have the highest income levels and homeownership rates of any Latino group. Within the latter two Latino
groups, there is also a racial divide, with black Cubans and
Puerto Ricans generally faring much worse than their
lighter skinned brethren.

Understanding the Asian population involves similar
decomposition. This is the most rapidly growing minority
population, up nearly 50 percent over the decade of the
1990s. In the most recent figures, Asian median household
income exceeds that of whites (this is partly because households often include multiple earners). College attendance
rates for eighteen- to twenty-one-year-olds are also well
above those of any other racial group. But the overall picture of social and economic health hides severe problems
for certain groups.

Figure 2-2 breaks down the Asian and Pacific Islander
population from the 2000 census.

**FIGURE 2-2. Composition of Asian and Pacific Islander
Population, 2000**

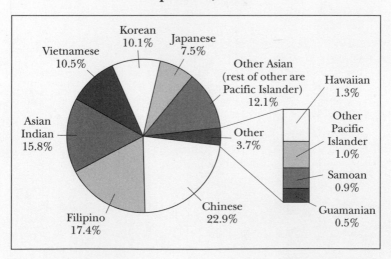

TABLE 2-3. Demographic Characteristics of U.S. Asian & Pacific Islander Populations, 1990

CHARACTERISTIC	Chinese	Filipino	Japanese	Asian Indian	Korean	Vietnamese
MIGRATION						
Percent U.S.-born Nationals	30.7	35.6	67.6	24.6	27.3	20.0
Percent Foreign-born Nationals	69.3	64.4	32.4	75.4	72.7	80.0
AGE						
Median Age of Selected Population	32.1	31.1	36.3	28.9	29.1	25.2
INCOME						
Per Capita Income (as % of Asian and Pacific Island avg.)	109.1	99.8	142.1	130.3	82.0	66.2
Poverty Rates for Individuals	14.0	6.4	7.0	9.7	13.7	25.7
EDUCATION						
Male: College Grad or Higher	46.7	36.2	42.6	65.7	46.9	22.3
Female: College Grad or Higher	35.0	41.6	28.2	48.7	25.9	12.2

CHARACTERISTIC	Hawaiian	Laotian	Cambodian	Thai	Hmong	Samoan
MIGRATION						
Percent U.S.-born Nationals	98.7	20.6	20.9	24.5	34.8	77.3
Percent Foreign-born Nationals	1.3	79.4	79.1	75.5	65.2	22.7
AGE						
Median Age of Selected Population	26.3	20.4	19.4	31.8	12.5	21.5
INCOME						
Per Capita Income (as % of Asian and Pacific Island avg.)	83.9	41.0	37.5	87.8	19.7	56.4
Poverty Rates for Individuals	14.3	34.7	42.6	12.5	63.6	25.8
EDUCATION						
Male: College Grad or Higher	13.0	7.0	8.6	47.7	7.0	9.8
Female: College Grad or Higher	10.7	3.5	3.2	24.9	3.0	6.1

Source: U.S. Dept. of Commerce, *We the Americans: Asians* and *We the Americans: Pacific Islanders,* Bureau of the Census, issued Sept. 1993

As can be seen, Chinese and Filipinos are the most populous national origin groups, with Asian Indians, Vietnamese, and Koreans the next most populous. This represents a significant shift from 1990, when Japanese-origin Asian Americans were the third most numerous group. The Indian and Vietnamese populations have made the most significant gains. Table 2-3 offers selected data on the Asian subgroups as of 1990; this is the latest year for which sufficiently detailed figures are available, and we list the groups in the order of their relative size as of that year.

Chinese and Filipinos, the largest groups, are largely foreign born with per capita income very close to the Asian American average; the Chinese, however, have a very high poverty rate, suggesting an extreme level of inequality within the community. Japanese Americans are now largely U.S. born—and boast the highest income levels of all the Asian groups. At the median, Asian Indians seem to be highly educated and high-earning newer immigrants. Koreans and Vietnamese are also newer immigrants, but education levels are lower, as is per capita income.

The Native American population may be the most challenged of all the major minority groups. If wealth formation is key to intergenerational upward mobility, then the taking of land and other assets from America's first residents has surely been a structural barrier. Table 2-4 offers a brief look at this diverse population. As can be seen, American Indians tend to be younger, less educated, and poorer.[3]

The poverty rate on reservations, often isolated from the major economic drivers of their states, is especially acute; in 1990, the rate was an appalling 50 percent. Native Americans also have the highest accident and suicide rates of any ethnic group.

Only about 20 percent of Native Americans live on reservations and trust lands, with another 15 percent in tribal jurisdiction or designated areas, and the vast remainder spread across the rest of the United States. The urbanization of Native Americans has been dramatic: while 13.4 percent of the Native American population lived in urban areas in

TABLE 2-4. Demographic Characteristics of Selected American-Indian Populations, 1990

CHARACTERISTIC	American Indian, Aleuts, & Eskimos	Total Population
AGE DISTRIBUTION		
Under 10 years old	20.5	14.7
10 to 19 years old	18.8	14.0
20 to 29 years old	17.4	16.2
30 to 39 years old	16.4	16.8
40 to 49 years old	11.4	12.7
50 to 59 years old	7.1	8.8
60 to 69 years old	4.8	8.3
70 years and over	3.7	8.5
FAMILY TYPE		
Married couple	64.2	78.6
Female householder, no spouse present	27.3	16.5
Male householder, no spouse present	8.5	4.9
EDUCATIONAL ATTAINMENT		
Percent High school graduate or higher	65.5	75.2
Percent Bachelor's degree or higher	9.3	20.3
Percent Graduate or Professional Degree	3.2	7.2
FAMILY INCOME IN 1989		
All Families	$21,750	$35,225
Married-couple families	$28,287	$39,584
Female householder, no husband	$10,742	$17,414
POVERTY RATES—1989 BY FAMILY		
Married-couple families	17.0	5.5
Male householder, no wife	33.4	13.8
Female householder, no husband	50.4	31.1
POVERTY RATES—1989 (PERSONS)		
All Reservations	50.7	13.1

	Total Population in thousands
POPULATION 1970–1990	
American Indians, Aleut & Eskimo Population	
1970	827
1980	1,420
1990	1,959
TEN LARGEST TRIBES	
Cherokee	308
Navajo	219
Chippewa	104
Sioux	103
Choctaw	82
Pueblo	53
Apache	50
Iroquois	49
Lumbee	48
Creek	44
TEN STATES WITH LARGEST POPULATION OF AMERICAN INDIANS, ALEUTS, AND ESKIMOS	
Oklahoma	252
California	242
Arizona	204
New Mexico	134
Alaska	86
Washington	81
North Carolina	80
Texas	66
New York	63
Michigan	56

Source: U.S. Dept. of Commerce, *We the . . . First Americans,* Bureau of the Census, issued Sept. 1993

1950, the figure in 1990 was 56.2 percent (Thornton, 2001). While part of the increase in the urban American Indian population was simply a rise in self-identification, federal programs were also launched to disperse people from reservations on the grounds that these areas offered few economic possibilities. With urbanization has come rising rates of intermarriage, and almost 60 percent of American Indians today are married to non-Indians (Thornton, 2001).

The trend toward increasing diversity cannot be ignored. Changes that were limited to the coasts are being realized everywhere. Soon, whites will no longer be the majority. What are the implications of these changes on the fundamental structure of opportunity in America? The country has reached a crucial juncture and, as people of color grow in number, it becomes even more imperative to reverse the pattern of inequity that has taken root and that undermines the nation's founding ideals. In moving forward, it is necessary to acknowledge and build on the achievements that have been made.

Accepting Diversity

Real progress has been made in achieving crossracial understanding and acceptance. The mass appeal of overt racism appears to be over. The most casual glance at the racial landscape seems to confirm this perception. The symbols and signs, both substantive and superficial, are everywhere. Hector Ruiz, child of a Mexican border town, is the chief operating officer (and CEO apparent) of Advanced Micro Devices—the main competitor of Intel. Kenneth Chenault, an African American, is chairperson and chief executive officer of American Express, one of the 100 largest companies in the United States with one of the most prestigious brand names in the world. Kim Ng, a Chinese American woman, is vice president and assistant general manager for the New York Yankees. She has handled numerous high-profile player contract negotiations. Ruth Simmons—the daughter of a Texas sharecropper and the first African American to

**Box 2-2. Youth Leading the Way
with a New Racial Attitude**

Confirming that today's youth are more accepting of racial and ethnic difference, a 1997 *USA Today*/Gallup poll of teenagers across the country ages thirteen to nineteen (Peterson, 1997) found that 57 percent of those who date said they have been out with someone of another race or ethnic group—white, black, Hispanic, or Asian. (Asians were not polled in this study.) Hispanic teenagers led the way, with 90 percent admitting they had been out with someone of a different race. Sixty percent of black teenagers and 47 percent of white teenagers said they had dated someone of another race. In addition, 36 percent of white teenagers and 28 percent of black teenagers who had not dated interracially said they would consider it. In 1980, the results of a similar poll by *USA Today* found that just 17 percent of teens said they had dated someone of another race.

For today's youth, race is clearly not a barrier to establishing friendships or going on a date. They are more relaxed and more open-minded about dating someone of a different ethnic group, an attitude that has no doubt been influenced by increased contact with others different from them in an increasingly multicultural world. Interracial dating is also supported by many parents, a separate *USA Today*/Gallup survey found, with 62 percent of parents saying they would be "totally fine" if their children dated interracially. When asked the reason why they would date someone of another race, the vast majority of teens—97 percent—said because they found the person attractive. Other reasons given included out of curiosity (75 percent), to be different (54 percent), and to rebel against parents (47 percent).

The survey showed, however, that some teens will never cross the racial line to date. It found that 43 percent of teenagers who date haven't dated interracially, and 13 percent said they never would. The survey also pointed out the continuing black-white divide, with 35 percent of nonblack teens who haven't dated interracially saying their parents would object if they dated a black teen compared with 20 percent whose parents would object to a white, a Hispanic, or an Asian teen. In addition, 24 percent of teens said white people would have a problem with a white teen dating a black teen, and 23 percent said black people would have a problem with a black teen dating a white teen. This compares to 8 percent of teens who said Asians would have a problem with an Asian teen dating a white teen. Furthermore, while only 1 percent of Hispanic teenagers said they would not consider interracial dating, 12 percent of black youth and 17 percent of white youth said they would not cross that line. Still, the survey found that the number of adults who agree with the statement "It's all right for blacks and whites to date each other" has risen from 48 percent in 1987 to 69 percent in 1997.

be president of a "Seven Sisters" college when she became president of Smith College in 1995—assumed the presidency of an Ivy League school, Brown University, in 2001. For two weeks in early 2001, Jennifer Lopez, a Puerto Rican, was the biggest pop icon in America: she had both the number-one album and the number-one movie in the country. One of today's most successful young media entrepreneurs is Christy Haubegger, the founder and publisher of *Latina* Magazine.

Workplaces are becoming more integrated; schools are increasingly multicultural. Studies show increased acceptance of racial and ethnic differences, with younger people socializing much more outside of their own racial groups (see Box 2-2).

Popular culture has never been more racially integrated. Hip-hop culture has created the kind of multiracial scene

that rock 'n' roll never did. Latino music is emerging as a
strong force. Hollywood's racial barriers have been significantly relaxed. Asian influenced cinema has broken out of
the art house. Sports figures, most of them black, are the
new superheroes: young people of every race, color, and
creed buy their sneakers, put their posters on the wall, and
follow their every move.

Intermarriages are also becoming more common. In
1994, 1.3 million intermarriages were reported, which is
four times the number reported in 1970 (Peterson,
1997). The majority of those unions—52 percent—are
between white Americans and Latinos; 19 percent are
between white Americans and Asian Americans; 12 percent
between white Americans and Native Americans; and 9
percent between white Americans and African Americans,
extrapolated from a chart published in the September 18,
2000, issue of *Newsweek*.

According to 1990 census data, 9.5 percent of the mar-
riages in Los Angeles County are crossracial, compared with
1.8 percent nationally, making interracial marriage five times
as prevalent. Using 1990 census data, David Hayes-Bautista,
director of the Center for the Study of Latino Health, examined the rate of intermarriage among younger couples in the
county, as he told PolicyLink staff in a conversation in February 2001. Of married couples less than twenty-five years old,
he found one-fourth of the married white Americans in Los
Angeles County were in an interracial marriage.

In past eras, much of the civil rights struggle focused on
guaranteeing rights, particularly those related to voting and
improving electoral outcomes. Progress in this arena has
been undeniable. In 1970, the Washington based Joint Center for Political and Economic Studies reported that there
were 1,469 black elected officials throughout the nation. By
1998, that figure had increased six-fold, to nearly 9,000. As
for Latinos, the National Association of Latino Elected and
Appointed Officials (NALEO) reports that there were 3,128
Latino elected officials in 1984; as of June 1999, there were
4,966—a nearly 60 percent increase over fifteen years.

While this electoral progress reflects the growing number of minority voters, white voters have also been more willing to cross racial lines while in the voting booth. There are many examples of elected African American leaders in largely white jurisdictions: Norm Rice, former mayor of Seattle; Harvey Gantt, former mayor of Charlotte, NC; J. C. Watts, member of Congress from Oklahoma. Latinos have also been successful in areas where the majority of voters are white, a crossover talent mastered because the disenfranchisement of immigrants and the younger age of the Latino population mean that Hispanic leaders frequently have to rely on Anglo votes to secure political office. A key example is Cruz Bustamante, a moderate Democrat who went from being speaker of the California Assembly to lieutenant governor in an election in which only 13 percent of the voters were Latino.[4]

While these victories of minority leaders in nonminority areas are a testament to the abilities of certain individuals to

FIGURE 2-3. Gallup Poll Results on the Social Acceptance of an African American President, 1958–1999

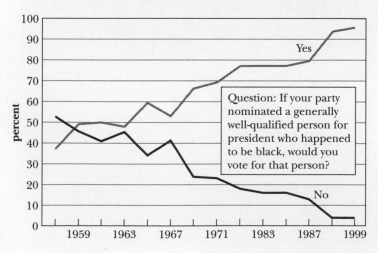

Question: If your party nominated a generally well-qualified person for president who happened to be black, would you vote for that person?

craft coalitions, growing acceptance is part of the story. As Figure 2-3 illustrates, the percentage of Americans that indicate that they would be willing to vote for a black president has risen from less than 40 percent in the late 1950s to more than 90 percent in the late 1990s.

Of course, when the voting curtains are drawn, many white Americans quietly refuse to endorse minority candidates, a fact pollsters factor in when predicting the outcome of elections (Reeves, 1997). Still, the shifts in attitudes have been profound.

Partly as a result of these shifts, both of the major political parties seem to have given up explicitly racist signals and statements. Even though a pro-minority stance has been more traditionally associated with the Democrats, the Republican National Convention of 2000 was a veritable pageant of multicultural America. And while President George W. Bush made no promises that his administration would "look like America," his cabinet has at least as many minority appointments as did the first cabinet of the Clinton administration.

Diversity, it seems, has become a sound political message. It is also becoming an accepted fact of business culture. Business magazines and leaders routinely discuss the value of a multiethnic work force as a way to reach new domestic and international audiences, with a 1999 *Fortune* study of the "50 Best Companies for Minorities" even touting the fact that these companies on the whole actually outperform their competitors.

Attitudes Are Mixed

In principle, whites have generally come to support equality and integration. In his comprehensive review of the available survey data, Lawrence Bobo (2001) reports that in the early 1940s, 68 percent of whites supported segregated schools, 54 percent supported segregated public transportation, and 54 percent favored job preferences for whites. Within twenty-five years, the percentages of whites taking these positions evaporated to the point where questions about public transportation and jobs need not be asked. By then, virtually all whites rejected segregated public transportation and job preferences for whites. Support for integrated schools proved to be a bit more stubborn, but by 1995, only 4 percent of whites expressed a preference for segregated schooling (Bobo, 2001). "[T]he positive trend among [w]hites on these principles across the domains of schools, public transportation, jobs, housing, politics, and even intermarriage is steady and unabated" (Bobo, 2001).

White Americans, however, have not embraced policy options offered to implement these principles. Bobo and Smith (1998) demonstrate how wide the gap between principle and implementation often is. In 1964, six out of ten white Americans supported the principle of school integration; by 1986, nine out of ten did. It was a different story when they were asked if the federal government should actively desegregate public schools. In 1964, perhaps not surprisingly, fewer than four out of ten thought the federal government had a role to play in the integration process. However, by 1986, even fewer whites—fewer than three in ten—supported taking action to realize the principle, even though virtually all of them supported it. That number has fallen even further since 1986 (Bobo, 2001). Similar patterns emerge in the areas of jobs and housing.

This soft support among whites for a proactive policy agenda is the result of a profound lack of information about today's realities about race. According to 2001 research conducted by the *Washington Post,* the Henry J. Kaiser Family Foundation, and Harvard University (Morin, 2001), large numbers of whites believe that blacks, as a whole, no longer suffer disproportionately from poverty. The poll found that "40 percent to 60 percent of all whites say that the average black American is faring about as well and perhaps even better than the average white" in the areas of jobs, incomes, schooling, and health care. As we will demonstrate in the next chapter, this is most certainly not the case. Because of the prevalence of this type of attitude, it is easy to see why there is little sense of urgency about solving racial inequality.

Whites also are holding on to some deep-seated prejudices about African Americans and Latinos. Utilizing 1990 General Social Survey (GSS) data, Bobo and Kluegel (1997) show that 54 percent of whites think blacks are not as intelligent, 62 percent think blacks are lazier, 56 percent think blacks are more violent, and 78 percent say blacks are more prone to prefer welfare when compared to whites (cited in Bobo, 2001). Latinos are similarly viewed, but Asians and Pacific Islanders are not (Bobo, 2001). Asians are saddled with a unique set of stigmas discussed later in this chapter.

As America becomes more diverse, some whites feel threatened. As one analyst noted, commenting on a *Miami Herald*/NBC-6 poll conducted in 1998, white non-Hispanics in South Florida are finding themselves "alienated" (Morgan, 1998). The frustrations of white Americans are being reflected in a backlash to affirmative action and their charges of "reverse discrimination."

Any discussion of racial attitudes would be incomplete without touching on the way people of color see themselves and each other. The 2000 census data show increasing numbers of people of color see themselves as of mixed race. In New Jersey alone, a state for which the data were released early, 213,755 respondents took advantage of the first-time opportunity to identify themselves as biracial (Associated Press, 2001).

People of color, because they are not monolithic, represent a diversity of views and perspectives. Within the Mexican American community, for example, tensions can exist between those with a long history in the country and recent arrivals (Campo-Flores, 2000). In analyzing the *Miami Herald*/NBC-6 poll, social scientists found that Cuban Americans expressed attitudes and high levels of satisfaction typically expressed by white non-Hispanics (Morgan, 1998). George Wilson, an assistant professor of sociology at the University of Miami, added that Cubans do not see racism as particularly widespread. That poll also indicated that the biggest perception gap exists between blacks and Cuban Americans, a notion buttressed by a separate *Miami Herald* article focusing on black Americans in South Florida who do not believe Cuban Americans are particularly sensitive to their long history of discrimination (Charles, 1998).

The sometimes divergent views of racial groups was demonstrated in the 1994 Los Angeles Survey of Urban Inequality, which states, "In many ways, the centerpiece of the modern racial divide comes in the evidence of sharply divergent beliefs about the current level, effect, and nature of discrimination." People of all races were asked if there was "a lot" of discrimination against blacks, Latinos, and Asians in getting well-paying jobs. Only about 23 percent of whites saw "a lot" of discrimination against either blacks or Latinos. More than two-thirds of both blacks and Latinos saw "a lot" of discrimination in their own circumstances. Interestingly, only about 40 percent of both blacks and Latinos saw "a lot" of discrimination in each other's situations. Asians are actually less likely than whites to believe that "a lot" of discrimination exists for either blacks or Latinos. Fewer than 10 percent of all groups saw "a lot" of discrimination against Asians, including Asians themselves (Bobo, 2001). It seems there is little consensus.

The various racial groups view immigrants in different ways, at least in California—often the harbinger of national trends. While a majority of Californians think positively about the contributions of immigrants, 45 percent of African Americans thought immigrants were a burden to the economy compared to 22 percent of Latinos. At the same time, 53 percent of the white population and 29 percent of Asians thought immigrants were a burden (Hajnal and Baldassare, 2001).

Defining Nature of the Black-White Paradigm

The mixed attitudes discussed above underscore that it will take a lot more soul searching, experimentation, forward steps, and backwards slipping before America comes to terms with its racial and ethnic dilemmas. America is a young country; it has been only 136 years since the end of the Civil War and barely more than one generation since the passage of the Civil Rights Act of 1965. Those in the first wave of students involved in forced busing in the early 1970s are just now thirty-something. No one should expect America to recover from 350 years of racism so quickly. Anyone familiar with the histories of ancient civilizations understands the historical insignificance of four decades. Remember, "by the middle of the twentieth century, the color line was as well defined and as firmly entrenched as any institution in the land. After all, it was older than most institutions, including the federal government" (Franklin, 1993).

In a time of increasing diversity, it might be tempting to look beyond the black-white framework that structures race relations and social and economic opportunity. To the contrary, as other racial minorities grow, it becomes increasingly important to address the fundamental question of fairness for African Americans, which affects the fortunes of the other groups. The black-white economic and social divide—created by slavery and cemented through years of servitude and subjugation—has endured and helped shape America. Even though the years before and during slavery witnessed unspeakable crimes of oppression inflicted upon Native Americans, "race in America took on a deeper and more disturbing meaning with the importation of Africans as slaves" (Hacker, 1992). Slavery demanded that black and white Americans coexist, forge intimate relationships, and share the most shameful acts of degradation, acts that both forged and damaged the psyche of the nation. Slavery set the rules, so to speak, for the etiquette of oppression and injustice. "If race figures so centrally in the life of the United States, it has much to do with the kind of country America is and has been from its start" (Hacker, 1992).

The fact is that the inferiority attributed to blacks has defined policy discussions as well as the way that other racial minorities are viewed. W. E. B. Du Bois (1903) foretold the

American predicament virtually a century ago: "The problem of the twentieth century is the problem of the color
line." Not even Du Bois could have appreciated the full
impact of his prediction today, notes John Hope Franklin
(1993). Gunnar Myrdal, a Swedish economist and social
reformer, called attention to the unique plight of African
Americans in his groundbreaking 1944 report, *An American
Dilemma: The Negro Problem and American Democracy*. Not only
did Myrdal find the unequal status and treatment of African
Americans a stain on the fabric of a country that proclaimed
the values of freedom, equality, and justice; he also noted a
uniqueness that applied only to African Americans. Of all
ethnic and racial groups, only African Americans were
thought to be "unassimilable" to the point that "amalgamation" with white Americans was intensely and staunchly pro-
hibited. While the Japanese and Chinese were also
considered "unassimilable" groups, this intensity of feeling
around "amalgamation" applied only to African Americans.

Twenty-four years later, the Kerner Commission (1968)
wrote that "[w]hat white Americans have never fully understood—but what the Negro can never forget—is that white
society is deeply implicated in the ghetto. White institutions
created it, white institutions maintain it, and white society
condones it."

Still, today these attitudes toward African Americans are
deeply ingrained. In *Rage of a Privileged Class*, Ellis Cose
(1993) relates a conversation he had with Ed Koch, former
mayor of New York, about the problems of Brooklyn's
Crown Heights neighborhood, a predominantly black community with a large Jewish presence. During the conversation, the former mayor remarked that the Jews think "the
city ought to give them a little credit" for staying in the
community when so many other white groups moved out.
"Why, I wondered as he talked, should any group get special credit for not maniacally shunning blacks? What kind
of a society have we created in which it is considered
acceptable to flee entire communities merely because members of another race move in?"

Racial prejudice against African Americans continues to shape the public policy agenda in subtle, and not so subtle, ways (Bobo, 2001). Myths about black people and black images stir debate about public policies, and when those policies are misguided, all Americans are hurt. For example, the stereotype of the single black mother as a long-term welfare recipient who would rather have another child than work her way off public assistance has driven welfare reform, even though most welfare recipients receive benefits for less than two years and are as likely to be white as black. The loss of the safety net for poor children hurts families of all races. The stereotype of black schoolchildren as rowdy and not interested in learning may have, subconsciously or not, resulted in the abandonment of the nation's public schools. This hurts all children, and no one is unaffected when the nation's youth are not afforded the proper skills to lead a productive life.

Because this country's understanding of race is polarized along the black-white axis, other groups are forced to make equally sharp distinctions. They are forced to define themselves in ways that are unnatural and perhaps uncomfortable to them. For example, outside of America, Asians do not identify themselves as a group but as Koreans, Japanese, Chinese, and so on. They are a multitude comprising over 30 ethnicities—ranging from fourth- and fifth-generation Chinese and Japanese Americans to more recent first-generation Southeast Asian refugees, and showing diverse and contrasting levels of affluence and poverty, education and literacy.

Similarly, Latinos, many of whom are of mixed race, would rather not lump themselves into one group, but must do so because of the context. As Juan Gonzalez (2000) writes, "[T]his country's stark black-white dichotomy is alien to Latinos. Rather, to varying degrees, based on the country of origin and even the region within the home country, ethnic identification, or nationality, remains more at the core of Latino identity." Even though the 2000 census offered Americans sixty-three racial categories from which to choose for self-identification, 42 percent of people nationwide who identified themselves as Latino on the census picked "other" as their racial category. In fact, 97 percent of the 15.4 million Americans who chose "other" were Latino. At the same time, 48 percent of people nationwide who identified themselves as Latino on the census picked "white" as their racial category (Martinez, 2001).

Both black and white Americans have long lost the opportunity to embrace the diversity within their communities. As slaves, blacks were stripped of all connection with their homelands so that today they are largely reduced to identifying with a continent rather than a country. Caribbean Americans of African origin do not necessarily consider themselves "African Americans." Neither do recent African immigrants. In denying African Americans their identity by treating them as a monolith, Anglo Americans, French Americans, Italian Americans, and Irish Americans were rendered simply "white." Often overlooked during discussions about the importance of diversity and preserving minority cultures is the fact that we have always been a nation of minorities. The heretofore white "majority" has never been a monolith either. When Americans reduce each other to a skin color, everyone gets diminished in each other's eyes.

To emphasize the significance of black inequality is not to argue that the black struggle for justice is more important than the struggle of others. Instead, it is a way to acknowledge that resolving the structural inequities that perpetuate the black-white divide is the key to unlocking the value of our increasingly diverse society. Over the past 150 years, the battles for justice for African Americans, including the movement for civil rights, have continued to inspire those who seek justice, fairness, and inclusion—notably women, members of other racial minorities, and gays. The African American struggle demonstrated that as blacks gain ground, so do all others in this mosaic that is America.

Embedded Nature of
the Black-White Paradigm

The embedded nature of inequality growing out of the black-white paradigm can be demonstrated by looking at two aspects of racial discrimination. First is the pattern of racial violence against blacks, which further stresses the entrenchment and widespread nature of antiblack sentiment. The other example—the persistent segregation of African Americans—even more vividly demonstrates the continuing discrimination that African Americans face.

In spite of its growing diversity and blurring of color lines, the United States remains racially segregated. Sunday morning, it is said, is perhaps the most segregated time in America—and few of even the most ardent integrationists question that. Despite all of the progress with school integration, the vast majority of white students do not go to school with many Asians, blacks, Latinos, or Native Americans.

**FIGURE 2-4. Hate Crime Incidents
as Reported to the FBI, 1995–1999**

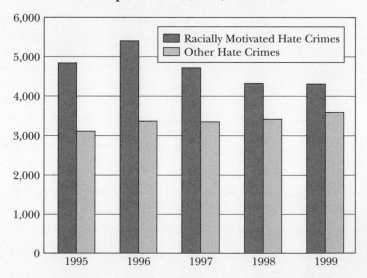

FIGURE 2-5. Racial Hate Crimes by Racial Group

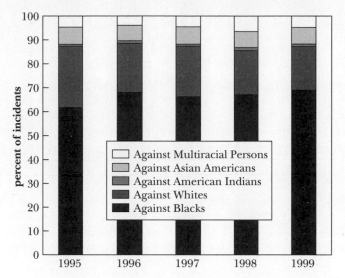

Racial violence against African Americans remains wide-spread. While the rate of hate crimes has recently waned, as Figure 2-4 shows, the proportion of hate crimes against blacks has been rising, as indicated in Figure 2-5, despite the fact that they are losing ground in population to other groups.

This is important because it demonstrates that, despite growing diversity, whites' attitudes toward blacks are what continue to sculpt the emotional landscape.

The pattern of racial violence that has grown out of the black-white paradigm is so completely embedded that when Asian Americans confronted their first widely publicized incidence of such violence in the modern age, they had to find a place on that racial polar axis. In 1982, Vincent Chin was killed in Detroit by autoworkers who were making anti-Japanese comments. In meetings, Asian American activists wrestled with the question of "[s]hould Asian Americans downplay race to stay in the 'safe' shadows of the white establishment? Or should they step out of the shadows and cast their lot with the more vulnerable position of minorities seeking civil rights?" (Zia, 2000). They probably did not have much of a choice. "In the end, we reached a consensus: to fight for what we believe in, we would have to enter the arena of civil rights and racial politics. Welcome or not, Asian Americans would put ourselves into the white/black race paradigm" (Zia, 2000).

On the policy front, while black-white housing segregation has lessened in recent years (for an analysis of 2000 census data, see Cohen and Cohn, 2001), the phenomenon persists. Black-white segregation has declined when measured by a so-called dissimilarity index—roughly the percentage of a group, say blacks, that would need to move so that they were evenly spread among the census tracts in a particular area (see Figure 2-6). Segregation of Latinos can be effectively tracked only from 1980 since prior to that time Latinos were usually identified in the census by surname or some other imprecise measure.

FIGURE 2-6. Black-White Segregation in Thirty Metropolitan Areas with Significant Black Population

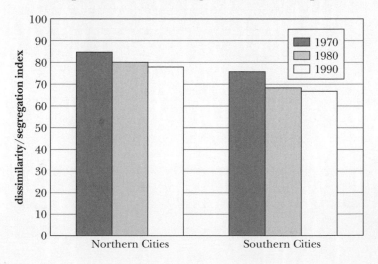

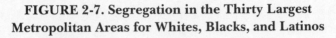

**FIGURE 2-7. Segregation in the Thirty Largest
Metropolitan Areas for Whites, Blacks, and Latinos**

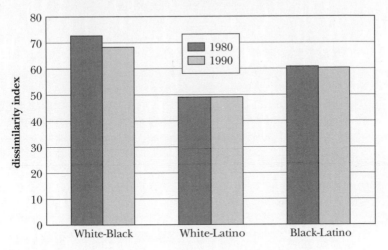

Figure 2-7[5] shows the pattern for the thirty most populous metropolitan areas in the United States: while black-white segregation has dropped, it is still much higher than Latino-white segregation.

Blacks and Latinos are more likely than blacks and whites to live together.

African Americans are more segregated than any other racial group. In addition, their segregation is not alleviated by wealth, as has been the case for every other ethnic and racial group. As Massey (2001) writes, "The most affluent blacks appear to be more segregated than the poorest Hispanics or Asians; and in contrast to the case of blacks, Hispanic and Asian segregation levels fall steadily as income rises, reaching low or moderate levels at incomes of $50,000 or more." Massey and Denton (1993) argue that residential segregation is at the heart of African American inequality: it undermines the social and economic well-being of blacks in the United States because it breeds concentrated poverty;

joblessness; educational failure; crime; social, geographic, and economic isolation; and a host of other ills.

The suburbanization of America in the 1950s and 1960s solidified segregation as white Americans left the cities in droves. Just as African Americans gained access to metropolitan areas long denied them, the value of those properties plummeted. As white people continued to leave cities and as more well-off African Americans spread out within cities, isolated neighborhoods of concentrated poverty and urban disinvestment proliferated. It is no coincidence that this movement for exclusion (the suburbanization of America)—supported by racially biased housing policies that kept African Americans out of the suburbs—came at the same time that civil rights leaders were mobilizing a movement of inclusion. The phenomenon of "white flight" to the suburbs has become a staple of the American landscape, and even though the most recent census data show that more minorities are moving to the suburbs, integration is not necessarily increasing. Chapter 5 further examines this key issue of suburban sprawl—one geographic manifestation of segregation and discrimination.

Moreover, a *Los Angeles Times* analysis (Fields, 2001) of 2000 census data suggests that segregation is spreading to Latinos and Asians, although there is disagreement on whether their situations parallel the experience of African Americans. Still, this is a troubling trend and points to the embeddedness of racial divisions in American society.

Limits of the Black-White Paradigm

If one solely regards the current racial order through the black-white racial lens, one would miss much of the picture. When Los Angeles exploded after the Rodney King verdict, for example, it was portrayed as "a [b]lack-[w]hite or perhaps a [b]lack-Korean affair; however, 51 percent of arrestees during the unrest were Latino and . . . Latinos were the single largest ethnic group (at 49 percent) in the neighborhoods damaged by the uprising" (Pastor, 1995).

Asians and Latinos have their own histories and therefore their own needs. Three quick examples come to mind:
immigrants, Latino poverty, and the particular social discrimination aimed at Asians.

Until recently, immigration was an issue that had not
veered off the black-white axis. After the Civil War, the
South needed rebuilding, and nonslave states had a continued need for cheap labor. The fact that no one wanted to
hire blacks precipitated a large wave of European immigration. Hundreds of thousands came from Germany, Ireland,
and Italy and, after periods of initial discrimination and
struggle, were eventually accepted as white Americans.

Chinese and Japanese workers were among the first
Asians to arrive in the country in the 19th century. At the
time, there was much discussion about where Asians fit in
relation to the Negro. San Francisco's *Daily Alta California*,
the most influential paper at the time, ran an editorial
arguing that the Chinese are "morally a far worse class to
have among us than the Negro" (Cose, 1992). Around the
same time, a state appellate court invalidated the conviction
of a white man who had killed a Chinese man because
blacks, mulattoes, and American Indians were not allowed
to provide evidence in court—and by extension, neither
were the Chinese, as in this case.

A change in immigration policy in 1965—precipitated by
the civil rights focus on inclusion—shifted the flow of immigrants coming to the United States, with many more people
coming from Asia and Latin America than from Europe.
President Lyndon B. Johnson insisted on an equality bill
that was a companion to the Civil Rights Act of 1965 that
curtailed efforts to keep people out of the country based on
race. This historic legislation set the stage for the increase in
diversity America is experiencing today (Cose, 1992).

As more foreign language speakers have joined the U.S.
population, questions have arisen about the appropriate
language of instruction in schools. The question of language
goes to the heart of identity, particularly for Latinos. Language issues prove that what constitutes a "racial issue" can-

not be confined to skin color. A black-white lens is not going to capture the nuances of the struggles of immigrants.

There are also nuances of Latino poverty that a black-white framework would not reach. Where black poverty tends to be characterized by the high incidence of joblessness, not so for Latinos. Mexicans are the working poor—high employment rates but generally earning below official poverty levels. Puerto Ricans, who are urban based and tend to mirror most the black community in being excluded from the job market, have high welfare rates and family disruption issues. In comparison, Cuban Americans often come from more privileged backgrounds, and that community has a strong support network for refugees. Each of these communities needs to be approached differently.

The black experience in America does not reflect the experiences of Asian Americans. For the Asian Pacific population, "minority" is not synonymous with "disadvantaged." Their experience and reality are complex (see Ong, 2000). Clearly, high levels of poverty mark many Asian communities, including the Vietnamese, Laotians, and Hmong, but many Asian groups are doing well economically. What, then, are the challenges?

Challenges may lie primarily in the area of social discrimination. Recent research suggests that even though the Asian population may be highly educated, the "rate of return" on education is lower for this group than it is for Anglos. While some of this may reflect the difficulty of gauging education's value when immigrants have received their degrees in another country, one study found that the returns are even lower for U.S.-born and less recent immigrants (see Pastor and Marcelli, 2001). The pattern suggests that Asian Americans may be experiencing problems with upward mobility—breaking through what has been termed the "glass ceiling" to the top of corporate and political leadership.

Asian Americans are often perceived as being "more foreign" than anyone else. Japanese Americans were interned during WWII but German Americans were not. Asian Americans have been viewed through many negative and limited lenses, but perhaps the most insidious stereotype is the more recent view of Asian Pacific Americans as the "model minority." Though seemingly positive in connotation, the term obscures a more accurate and complex depiction of Asian Americans, who suffer twice the poverty rate of white Americans (Ong et al., 1994). In some Asian American communities, the percentage of those living below the poverty level is nearly 50 percent (Ong and Hee, 1994). Asian Pacific Americans are not what the term "model minority" suggests.

Asian Pacific Americans are often used as scapegoats, pitted against other racial minorities. The term "model minority," expressed as if a compliment, shifts blame onto other minority groups, who become rhetorically leveraged as less than "model" in character, while downplaying the importance of a more thorough examination of the real discrimination and oppression experienced by Asian Americans.

Consider, for instance, the example of Korean American merchants in Los Angeles's Koreatown. In the 1992 riots following the Rodney King trial, Korean American lives were lost, and many of their stores were destroyed. In all, Asian American businesses suffered over $2 billion in damages. Many Asian Americans felt abandoned and invisible to the police, politicians, and policy makers. While the entire nation was forced to recognize some of the systemic levels of discrimination against African Americans through the verdict in the Rodney King trial, the interracial tension building between African and Asian Pacific Americans was not addressed. Instead, after the trial, Asian Americans were held up as the scapegoats of the dismal social conditions and frustrations in the inner city. After the violent explosion of civil unrest, there was only a limited acknowledgment of the biased structural social conditions wherein two minority groups were pitted against one another in the inner city: easy fodder for the media to discuss racial tensions, as if they were the cause of the rioting and frustrations, not the systemic oppression and lack of access to social advancement experienced by both groups.

More recently, in the 1996 presidential election campaign finance scandal, Asian Americans were stereotyped as dubious or unscrupulous donors by the media despite the widespread abuse of "soft money" contributions by corporate America. Asian Pacific Americans were tried, convicted, and exploited by the news media as the subversive and corruptive "new yellow peril" that threatened American democracy and political campaigns in this country with their connections to "Red China." After thousands of articles and newscasts, Asian Pacific Americans across the country waited for the protracted sensational media coverage to end, enduring outrage, betrayal, shame, and insult.

Conclusion

The nation is changing. All the implications of these changes will not be apparent for some time. Clearly, the country's increasing diversity demands that it take a much closer look at the persistent patterns of racial prejudice and inequality that continue to confront many people of color. The country must acknowledge and address the particular racial prejudice against African Americans that drives the structure of inequality in America. Growing diversity does not mean that racial justice has been achieved. The search for uncommon common ground continues. Chapter 3 examines in detail just how wide the gap is and the challenges that remain as the country strives toward racial justice.

Notes

[1] The calculations in these figures come from the results of the 1990 and 2000 census; for the 2000 census, we used the P.L. 94–171 Redistricting Data Summary File, using an algorithm to assign the mixed races numbers to distinct categories to maintain consistency with the 1990 calculations.

[2] The breakdowns for Latinos by national origin come from the 2000 census. The detailed breakdowns by age, etc., which are available in Tables 2-1 and 2-2, are the most recent figures from the *Current Population Surveys* of the U.S. census, a monthly sampling of the American population; the

reader will note that there is a slightly different breakdown by ethnicity in the tables because of the way the CPS collects data. The Latino population is of a sufficient size so that even a smaller sample can yield relatively reliable figures. This is not the case for Asians, and so in that discussion, we rely on the 2000 census numbers for the general breakdown by national origins but the 1990 census numbers for the detailed profile.

3 Snipp (1997) notes that part of the huge growth in the Native American population indicated in Table 2-4 is due to changing patterns of ethnic self-identification. See also Eschbach, Supple, and Snipp (1998).

4 See Hector Tobar, "In Contests Big and Small, Latinos Take Historic Leap," *Los Angeles Times*, November 5, 1998, p. A-1.

5 The measures of residential segregation in Figure 2-7 come from "The State of the Nation's Cities" (SNC)," a database that includes information on seventy-four of the country's largest cities and metro areas, with most variables drawn from the 1970, 1980, and 1990 censuses. SNC was compiled by Norman J. Glickman, Michael Lahr, and Elvin Wyly; it was initially assembled under HUD contract by the Center for Urban Policy Research to meet the data needs of the United Nations' Habitat II Conference held in Istanbul in June 1996 and has been expanded in variable coverage since. We specifically used version 2.11A (September 22, 1997) for both of these calculations and subsequent calculations in chapter 3 on the suburbanization of population and employment.

References

Associated Press. 2001. "Census Figures Indicate Melting Pot," March 8.

Bobo, Lawrence. 2001. "Racial Attitudes and Relations at the Close of the Twentieth Century." In Neil J. Smelser, William Julius Wilson, and Faith Mitchell, eds. *America Becoming: Racial Trends and Their Consequences*. Washington, DC: National Academy Press.

Bobo, Lawrence, and Ryan A. Smith. 1998. "From Jim Crow Racism to Laissez-Faire Racism: The Transformation of Racial Attitudes." In Wendy F. Katkin, Ned Landsman, and Andrea Tyree, eds. *Beyond Pluralism: The Conception of Groups and Group Identities in America*. Urbana and Chicago: University of Illinois Press.

Bobo, Lawrence, and J. Kluegel. 1997. "Status, Ideology, and Dimensions of Whites' Racial Beliefs and Attitudes: Progress and Stagnation." In Steven Tuch and James R. Martin, eds. *Racial Attitudes in the 1990s: Continuity and Change*. Westport, CT: Praeger. As quoted in Bobo (2001).

Campo-Flores, Arian. 2000. "Brown Against Brown." *Newsweek*, September 18.

Charles, Jacqueline. 1998. "Words, Deeds and Suspicions Hold Area's Neighbors Apart." *Miami Herald*, September 11.

Cohen, Sarah, and D'Vera Cohn. 2001. "Racial Integration's Shifting Patterns." *Washington Post*, April 2.

Cose, Ellis. 1993. *Rage of a Privileged Class*. New York: HarperCollins.

————. 1992. *A Nation of Strangers: Prejudice, Politics and the Populating of America*. New York: William Morrow and Company.

Davis, Mike. 2000. *Magical Urbanism: Latinos Reinvent the U.S. City*. New York: Verso.

Du Bois, W. E. B. 1903. *The Souls of Black Folk*. Chicago: A.C. McClurg & Co.; Cambridge, MA: University Press John Wilson and Son.

Eschbach, Karl, Khalil Supple, and C. Matthew Snipp. 1998. "Changes in Racial Identification and the Educational Attainment of American Indians, 1970–1990." *Demography*, Vol. 35, No. 1.

Fields, Robin, and Ray Herndon. 2001. "Segregation of a New Sort Takes Shape." *Los Angeles Times*, July 5.

Fix, Michael, and Wendy Zimmermann. 2000. *The Integration of Immigrant Families*. Washington, DC: The Urban Institute.

Fix, Michael, and Jeffrey S. Passel. 1994. *Immigration and Immigrants: Setting the Record Straight*. Washington, DC: The Urban Institute.

Fletcher, Michael A. 2000. "Growing Population Confronts Bias." *Washington Post*, October 2.

Franklin, John Hope. 1993. *The Color Line: Legacy for the Twenty-First Century*. Columbia, MO: University of Missouri Press.

González, Juan. 2000. *History of Empire: A History of Latinos in America*. New York: Penguin Books.

Hacker, Andrew. 1992. *Two Nations: Black and White, Separate, Hostile, Unequal*. New York: Charles Scribners' Sons.

Hajnal, Zoltan, and Mark Baldassare. 2001. *Finding Common Ground: Racial and Ethnic Attitudes in California*. San Francisco: Public Policy Institute of California.

Kerner Commission. 1968. *Report of the National Advisory Commission on Civil Disorders*. New York: Bantam.

Martínez, Anne. 2001. "New Choices on 2000 Census Fail to Offer Right Racial Fit for Many Latinos." *San Jose Mercury News*, May 25.

Massey, Douglas S. 2001. "Residential Segregation and Neighborhood Conditions in U.S. Metropolitan Areas." In Neil J. Smelser, William Julius Wilson, and Faith Mitchell, eds. *America Becoming: Racial Trends and Their Consequences*. Washington, DC: National Academy Press.

Massey, Douglas S., and Nancy A. Denton. 1993. *American Apartheid: Segregation and the Making of the Underclass*. Cambridge, MA: Harvard University Press.

Morgan, Curtis. 1998. "Cultural Divide is Testing Ground for the Nation." *Miami Herald*, May 3.

Morin, Richard. 2001. "Misperceptions Cloud Whites' View of Blacks." *Washington Post*, July 11.

Myrdal, Gunnar. 1944. *An American Dilemma: The Negro Problem and American Democracy*. New York: Harper & Brothers.

Ong, Paul M. 2000. "The Asian Pacific American Challenge to Race Relations." In Paul M. Ong, ed. *The State of Asian Pacific America: Transforming Race Relations*. Los Angeles: Leadership Education for Asian Pacifics, Inc. (LEAP) Asian Pacific American Public Policy Institute and UCLA Asian American Studies Center.

Ong, Paul, Edna Bonacich, and Lucie Cheng. 1994. "Capitalist Restructuring and the New Asian Immigration." *The New Asian Immigration in Los Angeles and Global Restructuring*. Philadelphia: Temple University Press.

Ong, Paul M. and Suzanne J. Hee. 1994. "Economic Diversity." In Paul Ong, ed. *The State of Asian Pacific America: Economic Diversity, Issues & Policies*. Los Angeles: Leadership Education for Asian Pacifics, Inc. (LEAP) Asian Pacific American Public Policy Institute and UCLA Asian American Studies Center.

Pastor, Jr., Manuel. 2001. "Economics and Ethnicity: Poverty, Race, and Immigration in Los Angeles." In Marta López-Garza and David R. Diaz, eds. *Asian and Latino Immigrants in a Restructuring Economy: The Metamorphosis of Los Angeles*. Stanford, CA: Stanford University Press.

———. 1995. "Economic Inequality, Latino Poverty, and the Civil Unrest in Los Angeles." *Economic Development Quarterly*, Vol. 9, No. 3.

Pastor, Jr., Manuel, and Enrico Marcelli. 2001. "Men N the Hood: Spatial, Skill, and Social Mismatch for Male Workers in Los Angeles." *Urban Geography*, forthcoming.

Peterson, Karen S. 1997. "For Today's Teens, Race 'Not an Issue' Anymore." *USA Today*, November 3.

Reeves, Keith. 1997. *Voting Hopes Or Fears?: White Voters, Black Candidates & Racial Politics In America*. New York: Oxford University Press.

Snipp, C. Matthew. 1997. "Some Observations About Racial Boundaries and the Experiences of American Indians." *Ethnic and Racial Studies*, Vol. 20, No. 4.

Thornton, Russell. 2001. "Trends Among American Indians in the United States." In Neil Smelser, William Julius Wilson, Faith Mitchell, eds. *America Becoming: Racial Trends and Their Consequences*. Washington, DC: National Academy Press.

Yeoman, Barry. 2000. "Hispanic Diaspora." *Mother Jones*, July/August.

Zia, Helen. 2000. *Asian American Dreams: The Emergence of an American People*. New York: Farrar, Straus and Giroux.

3

American Progress and Disconnection

The contemporary United States presents a conundrum. On the one hand, the civil rights movement and its aftermath have brought tremendous progress. African Americans, once enslaved and then subjected to Jim Crow laws, have made sustained inroads into both the professions and the arts. Latinos, early victims of land takings in the Southwest and legal discrimination there and elsewhere, have risen to prominent political positions in California, Texas, Florida, and other states where they constitute a rapidly growing constituency. Asian Americans, previously explicitly excluded from immigrating to the United States, are now disproportionately represented in institutions of higher learning and enjoy, on average, median household incomes that exceed those of white Americans. Native Americans, a group first displaced then systematically isolated from the U.S. mainstream, have developed vibrant gaming industries that are contributing to reservation coffers.

At the same time, continuing problems abound. African American and Latino incomes still lag well behind those of white Americans, with high rates of joblessness a driving factor for one group, and severe conditions of working poverty the leading explanation for the other. In general, Asian Americans enjoy educational advantage but also suffer from poverty rates that are twice those experienced by white America; this is partly because poverty is a function of household size as well as income, but it is also because there are significant pockets of poverty in certain Asian communities, particularly recent immigrants. Meanwhile, many Native Americans remain mired in economic and social despair, whether on reservations or in major cities.

The persistent gap between the fortunes of whites and people of color is only part of the story. Income inequality, on the rise within the country as a whole, has been especially acute within the African American and Latino populations—a consequence of rising levels of concentrated poverty brought on by the departure of the more connected African Americans and Latinos from central cities.

This chapter explores the continuing differences by race in economic indicators such as income, wealth, and labor market experiences both between minority groups and white Americans, and within minority groups themselves. Despite the bleak picture, there are some bright spots, especially the striking increase in minority entrepreneurship over the past decade. But the general picture suggests that the gains since the 1960s have not been sufficient to take low-income people out of poverty. The future also looks problematic, particularly if one focuses on the one-third of black and Latino children growing up below the poverty line, the sharp differences in wealth (which, after all, affords advancement) between white and minority Americans, and the persistent "redlining" that prevents minority businesses from getting their fair share of financial credit.

Why the dispiriting pattern? Discrimination continues to play a role in both job markets and housing; even studies of minority executives and professionals report difficulties in making progress through corporate hierarchies, and lower-skill workers often find it hard to get past the interview process. But the more important culprits in contemporary inequity may be factors bequeathed by a legacy of racialized housing, labor market, and educational policies—uneven opportunities for quality schooling, high concentrations of the ethnic poor, and limited social networks. Tackling these issues will require the caution of nuance: as was made clear in chapter 2, there are important differences among and within minority groups that mean that no one-size policy will fit all communities.

But the country must tackle them if it is to go beyond the embrace of diversity and instead make real changes in the material realities that structure the life chances of people of color. The goal of this chapter is to provide an informed base for these considerations; subsequent chapters identify the principles that work for achieving racial equity, then explore the complex policy challenges ahead and the leadership that will be required to confront them with both honesty and courage.

The Economy and Race

Some years ago, David Ayon of Loyola Marymount College was a participant in a college session on race and racism. When the students in the audience, earnest in their curiosity about how to bridge racial differences, turned to him, he made a remark that recalled *Guess Who's Coming to Dinner*—the famous 1960s movie with Sidney Poitier—and that stunned his listeners: "I don't really care whether you invite me over to your house for dinner. I want to own a house."

The challenge is indeed how to move forward from the acceptance of diversity to the achievement of social justice. Of course, diversity and justice can be connected. For example, psychological researchers have argued that intergroup contact tends to diminish prejudice, paving the way for a caring about "the other" that can, one hopes, provide the coalitional material for achieving equality. At the same time, few people want to arrive at the table as a junior partner, particularly since junior partners are often ignored; as a result, insuring that minorities make solid economic and political progress is key to "persuading" others at more diverse tables to learn truly the virtues of acceptance.

What has actually happened in this balance between psychological attitudes and material progress? While acceptance has increased, as chapter 2 has noted, relative economic conditions have stagnated. Figure 3-1 charts the performance of median family income from 1947 to 1999, adjusted throughout to reflect 1999 dollars.

While the gains of the civil rights movement did increase the median income of African American families, they were not enough to offset a widening gap in the median family income between black and white Americans. After the early 1970s, American statisticians began recognizing that the world was not simply two-toned, and data became available on Latinos and Asians—and since many Latinos count themselves as white in racial if not ethnic terms, the phrase

FIGURE 3-1. U.S. Median Family Real Income by Race and Hispanic Origin, 1947–1999, in 1999 Dollars

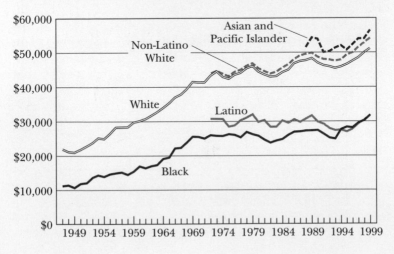

non-Hispanic white or "Anglo" came into common use.[1] As can be seen, the newly identified Latino families have fared poorly in recent years, with incomes falling to the levels of African Americans. Meanwhile, median Asian American family income has actually tracked slightly above that of the median for white Americans.

Figure 3-2 focuses on the more recent period from 1972 to 1999 and on median *household* income, once again adjusted for inflation. In this chart, all groups post lower incomes, primarily because this count includes nonfamily households consisting of one individual or nonrelated member, with the former especially likely to have lower incomes.

However, in relative terms, Asians do even better in this category, while Latinos and African Americans share the bottom of the income distribution; note further that Latino income has slipped over the years, becoming nearer African-American household income. The bottom line: excluding

FIGURE 3-2. U.S. Median Household Real Income by Race and Hispanic Origin, 1972–1999, in 1999 Dollars

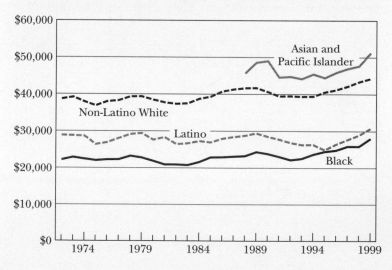

Asians, there is virtually no closing of the racial economic gap. The divide actually seems to have widened from the mid-1990s onward, and the economic outcomes for African Americans and Latinos are growing more parallel.

The Lines of the Divide

Why the divergence in income? One factor is simply the relatively high levels of unemployment experienced by the largest U.S. minority groups. As illustrated in Figure 3-3, black and Latino unemployment is consistently higher than that experienced by white Americans.

Two trends, however, are worth noting. First, over time, the African American and Latino unemployment rates have been converging. Second, the gap between the experience of these groups and white Americans grows in a recession (such as the mid-1970s, early 1980s, and early 1990s); conversely, blacks and Latinos benefit significantly when there

FIGURE 3-3. Unemployment Rates by Race/Ethnicity, 1973–2000

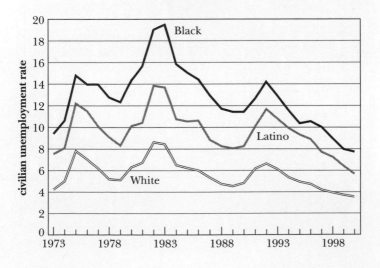

is a sustained recovery, as in the latter part of the 1990s. This signals an important issue raised by Harvard sociologist William Julius Wilson and others, which we will discuss in chapter 5: despite the fact that it seems like a neutral or even technical topic, sustaining economic growth is a key part of any civil rights agenda.

Growth, however, does not correct all problems. Despite the fact that unemployment rates of whites, blacks, and Latinos were converging in 1998–2000, there was still a large differential in household income. The reason: differences in the incomes of those who do work. Figures 3-4 and 3-5 show the usual weekly earnings of male and female full-time workers, respectively.

Several points are clear. First, the gap between the earnings of white and African American males has been remarkably persistent: the only moments when it has really narrowed have been at the end of a long boom of growth, as in the early 1970s and the late 1990s. Second, the much-

FIGURE 3-4. Median Usual Weekly Earnings of Male Full-Time Workers, 1967–1999

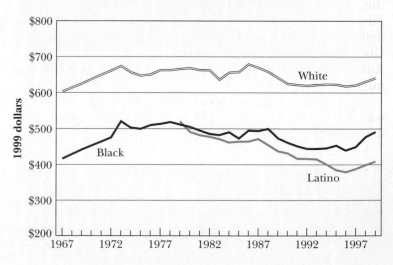

**FIGURE 3-5. Median Usual Weekly Earnings
of Female Full-Time Workers, 1967–1999**

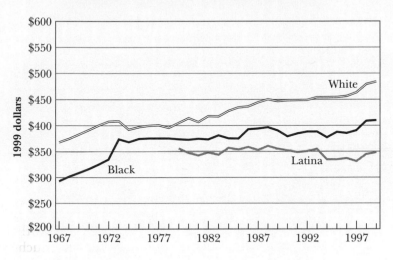

ballyhooed closing of the economic gap between white and African American women was true through the 1970s, but the difference widened during the 1980s and 1990s. Finally, Latino incomes for full-time workers have been drifting steadily away from the earnings of other groups. Given that Latino *household* income actually exceeds that of African Americans, this suggests that Latino homes have many wage earners.

The combination of higher unemployment and lower wages leads inevitably to higher poverty rates. Figure 3-6 illustrates the long-term trends.

Despite the relative lack of movement in median household income noted earlier, there was in fact dramatic progress in reducing the black-white poverty differential through the 1960s. The reasons were straightforward: the new opportunities wrought by the struggle against discrimination and the long economic boom of the 1960s. The gap between blacks and whites, however, was quite persistent

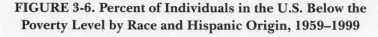

FIGURE 3-6. Percent of Individuals in the U.S. Below the Poverty Level by Race and Hispanic Origin, 1959–1999

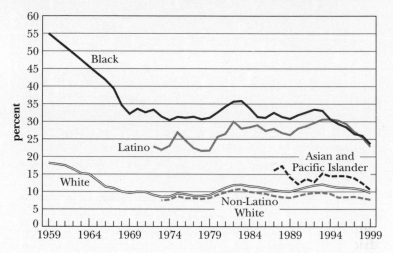

through the 1970s and 1980s; not until the long recovery of the 1990s do we see African Americans once again making relative gains.

The 1990s also brought another phenomenon: for the first time, Latino poverty actually exceeded (and then equaled) African American poverty. (This is not inconsistent with the finding that Latinos have higher household incomes than African Americans because poverty depends on household size as well as income.) While the reasons for growing Latino poverty are complex, part of the cause lies in the increasing presence of foreign-born Latinos, many of whom work for lower wages and often directly compete with U.S.-born Latinos in working-class occupations that occupy the lower tiers of the American economy. As for Asians, while the "model minority" stereotype persists, Asian Americans actually have a poverty rate much higher than that of Anglos—a fact that suggests that higher household and family incomes are partly driven by the sheer size of Asian households.

Will Differences Persist?

After looking at the dismal pattern previously described, one might hope that at the least the future will bring improvement. There are, unfortunately, good reasons to be worried rather than hopeful. Figure 3-7, for example, shows the poverty of children—one of the standard predictors of academic performance and, therefore, of future earnings.

The figures are shocking: well over one-third of all African American and Latino children and nearly 20 percent of Asian American children live below the poverty line, a striking turn for a country that supposedly values its youth. Part of the reason for the higher rates affecting African Americans and Latinos is the extraordinarily high

FIGURE 3-7. Child Poverty Rate by Race, Average for 1996–1999

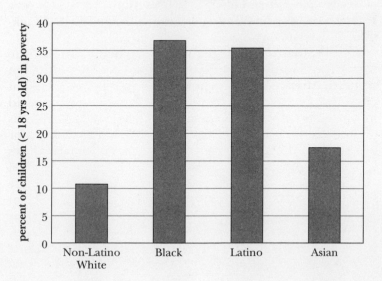

rates of female-headed households. As can be seen in Figure 3-8, the total percentage of children living in female-headed households has been rising, but the percentage of children below poverty who live in such households has been increasing even more dramatically.

Female-headed households tend to have lower incomes than male-headed households, primarily because of the occupational clustering of women and lingering discrimination in pay as well as the difficulties of holding full-time employment while being the sole provider of income, childcare, and supervision. As Figure 3-9 illustrates, this set of challenges is far more likely to have an impact on black families: while the past few years have brought some increase in the percentage of black children living in two-parent households, significantly more are living with only their mother, only their father, or in other living arrangements.

FIGURE 3-8. Percent of Total Related Children in Female Householder Families, by Poverty Status: 1959–1999

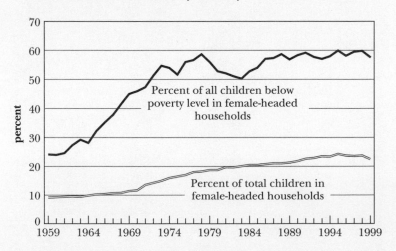

FIGURE 3-9. Children in Black Families, 1968–1998

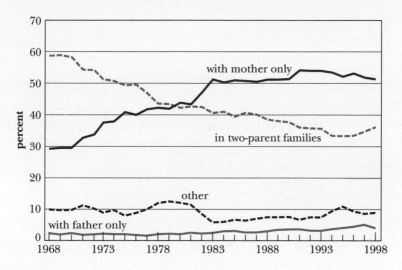

The consequences for life chances when growing up under such conditions are problematic. One immediate challenge is health. As Figure 3-10 illustrates, while less than 9 percent of white children lack access to health insurance, nearly 30 percent of Latino children remain uncovered. While access to healthcare is important, it is only part of the story: as Figure 3-11 illustrates, Latino infant mortality is quite close to that of white infant mortality, in spite of high poverty and limited health insurance, suggesting an underlying basis of health that has often been stressed by UCLA professor David Hayes-Bautista (see, for example, Hayes-Bautista, 1993).

However, the black-white gap is significant—and other risks along the way, including the high rates of death by homicide discussed in chapter 5, lead to very large gaps in life expectancy among the groups (see Figure 3-12).

As Melvin Oliver and Tom Shapiro (1995) have noted in their path-breaking book *Black Wealth, White Wealth*, one's

FIGURE 3-10. Health Insurance Access in America by Race, 1999

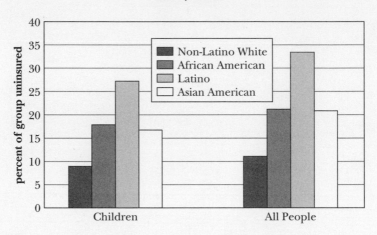

FIGURE 3-11. Infant Mortality Rates by Race, 1983–1996

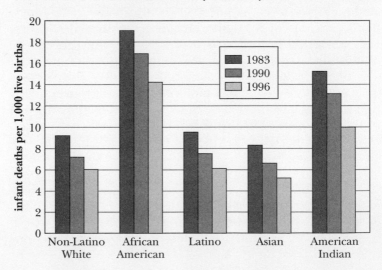

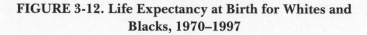

FIGURE 3-12. Life Expectancy at Birth for Whites and Blacks, 1970–1997

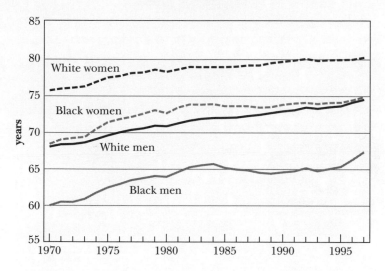

broader chances in life—not just for survival but for success—are really determined not by income but by wealth or assets, particularly since wealth can be passed on from generation to generation. As Figure 3-13 shows, huge gaps by race remain in homeownership, a traditional indicator of wealth.

Latinos did manage to post dramatic gains, but African Americans actually slipped in 1998 after modest growth through the 1980s; white Americans, meanwhile, made steady gains on their already high figures.

In his book *Being Black, Living in the Red*, Dalton Conley (1999) argues that this wealth difference represents the concrete legacy of racial inequality, including differential access to loans because of "redlining" (ACORN, 2000) as well as steering of minority home buyers, particularly blacks, to less desirable neighborhoods. Such a wealth gap "is not easily remediable because it largely results from past dynamics rather than from a dearth of 'equal opportunity' in the post-

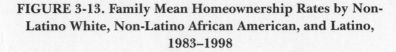

FIGURE 3-13. Family Mean Homeownership Rates by Non-Latino White, Non-Latino African American, and Latino, 1983–1998

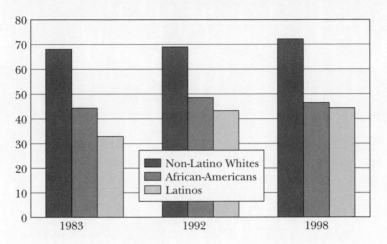

1960s world" (Conley, 1999), that is, assuming that ending discrimination would create equal incomes is misplaced, given the differences in basic assets and how this then alters the set of opportunities facing different Americans.

Indeed, as Figure 3-14 indicates, the playing field is nowhere near level: financial wealth apart from home equity—the wealth that begets more wealth by virtue of interest, dividends, and accumulation—is even more unequally distributed than is homeownership.

Moreover, while all groups have gained over the past two decades, African Americans are falling behind in relative terms. For Latinos, the relatively strong improvement over the 1980s was actually followed by a slump in financial gains during the long boom of the 1990s. In short, while social attitudes regarding minorities have changed dramatically in the past few decades, material progress has been far more paltry, and an analysis of future prospects suggests more of the same.

FIGURE 3-14. Family Mean Financial Wealth by Non-Latino White, African American, and Latino, 1983–1998 (in 1998 Dollars)

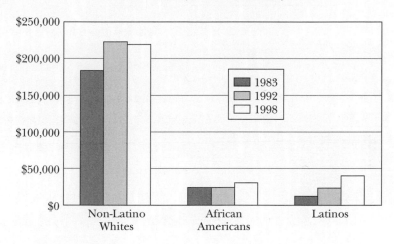

Of the many challenges that comprise the new frontier for racial issues, closing the economic gap is paramount. Forward movement in this area should make it easier for minorities to improve neighborhood, health, and other outcomes. But progress will also be made by recognizing the complexity of factors behind the persistent inequalities.

The first step in complicating the story is a recognition that some members of minority groups have done very well in the past thirty years. Figure 3-15 charts the Gini coefficient—a measure economists use when considering inequality that ranges between zero for "perfect equality" (if all households had the same income) and one for "perfect inequality" (if one family received all the nation's income).

In fact, while inequality has been on a long-term rise for all groups in the United States, inequality *within* the black population has consistently been higher than in the white community. Latino in-group inequality is a bit lower, but its

FIGURE 3-15. Income Inequality Within Racial Groups by Household, 1972–1998

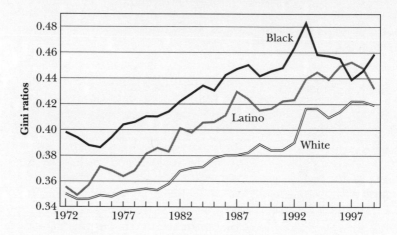

rate of increase is exceeding that of black Americans or white Americans.

African Americans and Latinos are, in short, even more bifurcated by income than Anglos; the booming economy has spelled opportunity for some but distress for many others. The reasons are complex—having to do with many being left behind in the central city while select others enjoy business and corporate success—but the consequence of this separation of economic fates is severe and affects both white Americans and people of color.

First, because there are examples of success, a combination of complacency and blame can take root. When some individuals do seem to "make it," particularly in highly visible fields, it is easy to suggest that discrimination has faded and that the remaining disparities may, in fact, be due to differences in talent, ambition, and skills. This view imagines away the effects of structural discrimination in terms of uneven educational opportunities, unstable family incomes, undesirable spatial locations, and other factors that make it difficult for children and parents to realize their dreams. Rather than assuming that the exception proves the rule, society needs to contemplate the average or usual experience for many people of color.

The second consequence of the separation of economic fates is evident in minority communities themselves. In an earlier era, the strictures of housing segregation (housing discrimination) forced the black and Latino middle class to remain within confined, largely minority areas. While the prevention of mobility had negative effects, including limited opportunities to gain home equity and personal wealth, it also forced a particular cross-class character to many urban minority communities, ensuring a diversity of leadership and income levels that often provided stability to neighborhoods as well as connections to employment. Inner-city communities of today have been left without those stabilizing influences as middle-class blacks and Latinos have moved to housing opportunities in the suburbs. The challenge for urban reformers is restoring a sense of stability and hope to those isolated inner-city neighborhoods and connecting their residents to the economic mainstream. Some of the strategies for combating inner-city decay and re-creating stable mixed-income communities are noted in chapter 5 under a policy discussion of urban sprawl. These are the kinds of strategies that are sorely needed to reduce the economic gap that exists within minority communities.

Minority Small Business: A Bright Spot

Despite the general lack of forward movement on income and wages, there has been one bright spot on the economic horizon: the growth of minority business. The number of black owned firms increased 108 percent from 1987 to 1997, well above the 27 percent national rate of growth in the number of all businesses. Hispanic owned firms increased even more rapidly over the period (232 percent), while the number of Asian owned firms rose by 180 percent. The proclivity to form enterprises can be seen through the prism of another statistic: while the number of white Americans who were self-employed went up 1.1 percent between 1982 and 1998, the number of black Americans who were self-employed rose by 28.7 percent, with a corresponding 30.1 percent rise for Hispanics and a striking 56.5 percent increase for Asians. Perhaps having sensed little room for upward mobility in traditional employment, many minorities are deciding to strike out on their own.

The growth in the revenues of these minority enterprises has been even more striking: Asian owned businesses experienced a 463 percent increase from 1987 to 1997, with a 417 percent increase for Hispanic owned firms, and a 109 percent increase for black owned firms. When compared to the growth in the number of firms, average revenues are found to be essentially flat for black owned firms but doubled for Latino firms and more than doubled for Asian enterprises. Part of the reason that Asian and Latino owned firms are growing faster is that these firms are exploring new niches, particularly exports based on immigrant ties to home countries. Along with black owned firms, they are also servicing the "new urban markets" (such as in ethnic foods) made possible by the significant presence of people of color in America's densely populated central cities.[2]

Despite the impressive growth figures, minority firms are still underrepresented: African Americans, for example, were 12.5 percent of the population in 1997, but black owned firms were only 4 percent of all firms, with the comparable figures for Latinos being 11 percent of the population and 5.8 percent of the firms. In short, one reason why the percentage growth is so high for minority enterprise is that the base was low to begin with. Moreover, the majority of minority firms are very small: in 1997, for example, 40

percent of Latino owned firms had receipts of less than
$10,000; average annual receipts for Latino owned busi-
nesses were slightly over $155,000, well below the nearly
$900,000 average for all firms. Indeed, many minority
firms are essentially arrangements of self-employment:
while 25 percent of the Asian owned firms had employees,
only 14 percent of the Hispanic firms and 10 percent of the
black owned firms hired outside workers.[3]

Even at this modest scale, however, minority companies
can be good for equity and community development. A
1995 survey of the black owned businesses in the Atlanta
metropolitan area, for example, found that 24.6 percent of
the employees in black owned firms in the city of Atlanta
came from low-income, inner-city neighborhoods; even
black owned businesses in suburban areas of Atlanta drew
nearly 20 percent of their employees from low-income
neighborhoods (Boston, 2001). Harvard Business School
professor Michael Porter, famous for having explored the
competitive advantage of nations, is now touting the
growth opportunities for minority owned, inner-city firms
and arguing that they are a key part of neighborhood revitalization (Porter, 1995). In short, efforts that focus on
encouraging the establishment of minority owned businesses may be viable ways to promote workforce and community development for people of color.

Such efforts may also help the nation's overall economic
scenario, partly given the key role of small business in driving America's "new economy." The Milken Institute, usually concerned with broad economic trends, recently
released a report focusing on minority business. The
authors note that "absent broad-based institutional investor
participation in minority and immigrant business communities . . . continued growth in the American economy is
impossible, affecting not just minority businesses but [also]
putting the nation's macroeconomy at risk" (Yago and
Pankrantz, 2000).

To realize the potential, certain key issues will need to be
addressed. For example, while the small scale of minority

enterprise partly reflects a tendency to concentrate in the service sector, another limit on business growth is the "redlining" described earlier: nearly 37 percent of all businesses use bank credit, but the figure for minority businesses is 27 percent, with an especially low 15 percent for black owned businesses. One study found that, controlling for the usual factors used to judge creditworthiness, Latino firms were 12 percent more likely to be denied credit, while black firms were twice as likely to be turned down (Cavalluzo and Cavalluzo, 1998). The Milken report also suggests that there is a significant gap on the venture capital side, linking this in part to the separate social networks of minority owners and the larger venture investors.

Moreover, analyses of the longest-running firms owned by blacks suggest that minority procurement programs have been critical to gaining the experience needed to compete in the open market. However, the legal environment for such programs has become problematic, despite the fact that such programs do seem to be effective at generating faster growth in minority enterprises (Boston, 2001). With credit still denied and key tools for advancement taken off the table, one has to be doubly impressed by the entrepreneurial spirit now sweeping ethnic America—and wonder how much more could be accomplished in building individual and community wealth should policy leaders and financial lenders become more supportive.

The Driving Factors of Inequality

In considering the persistent patterns of inequality just highlighted, one is immediately driven to wonder why. One factor is discrimination. While the popular notion is that most egregious abuses of racial preferences were eliminated by civil rights legislation, clear evidence of discrimination remains at the job and elsewhere. There are, of course, the dramatic statistics on credit denial and wealth accumulation presented earlier in the chapter—a trend that constrains the full potential of minority entrepreneur-

ship. But discrimination persists in labor and housing markets as well.

A telling new study of employers' preferences, for example, suggests that black males continue to face an often
unspoken skepticism in the hiring process, partly because
of employer presumptions that younger African Americans
lack the "soft skills"—workplace habits of promptness,
courtesy, teamwork, and willingness to learn—that have
become increasingly important in the contemporary workplace (Moss and Tilly, 2001). A 1998 study by recruitment
firm Korn/Ferry International suggests that the problem is
not limited to the lower echelons of the workplace hierar-
chy. Nearly 60 percent of minority senior-level executives
reported observing a double standard in assignments or
harsh and unfair treatment of minorities, with the problems most severe for blacks and less so for Asians. The consequences of this disparity in treatment are quite real: the
U.S. Department of Labor's Glass Ceiling Commission
reported that fewer than 3 percent of the top-level managers in the nation's largest firms is minority.[4]

Discrimination in housing also remains a serious issue.
Various "matched pair" tests—in which white and minority
testers adopt similar background profiles to search for
houses and observe for instances of discrimination—still
yield evidence of steering by realtors.[5] The continuing patterns of residential segregation, albeit lessened from earlier
decades, attest to this process. Meanwhile, social discrimination, including racial profiling by the police, continues to
be a disturbing presence on the American scene.

But overt discrimination by whites in employment and
housing cannot fully explain the patterns, particularly
given the evidence of attitudinal shifts and the long-term
change in the legal climate regarding civil rights. While
individual decisions to discriminate are important, key
structural barriers to equality also remain, from the spatial
mismatch that lands many minorities far away from
employment to the disparities in computer access that
result as much from income as from race. Tackling the con-

tinuing disparities in social and economic opportunities requires new policies and strategies that are focused on achieving equity. Chapter 5 examines in more detail some of the emerging solutions to these persistent problems.

One key factor in the inequality is that there are large educational differences among groups, accounting for some but not all of the differences in economic outcomes. To the extent that the educational gap is created by uneven access to quality education, aggressive policies should be developed. The mood in the country with regard to this is positive, with both Republicans and Democrats seeming to agree that targeting low-income minority schools is necessary. There is significant disagreement, however, on the mix of funding, testing, and parental choice that will help these schools improve their performance and the life chances of children in them. Still, the renewed focus on education has the potential to reduce inequalities later in life, and the consensus on targeting is heartening.

Geography is also crucially important. In his seminal book, *Poverty and Place,* Paul Jargowsky documents the increase in the concentration of poverty, particularly among people of color, in U.S. metropolitan areas. Defining concentration as living in a census tract where over 40 percent live below the poverty line, he finds that 34 percent of all poor African Americans, 22 percent of all poor Latinos, and only 6 percent of all poor whites live in such resource-scarce neighborhoods in metropolitan areas (Jargowsky, 1997). As a result, while African Americans and Latinos comprise less than 24 percent of the total U.S. population living in metropolitan areas, they are over 80 percent of those living in high-poverty conditions in urban America.

This geographic isolation or concentration is not accidental. As Massey and Denton (1993) argue, racial discrimination in housing markets, which allowed whites an easier exodus from the city than people of color, contributed to the problem: since blacks are more likely to be poor, boxing in communities through segregation will necessarily generate an increase in the concentration of poverty. This was, Massey and Denton stress, not simply a matter of private choice, with individuals choosing in the free market to enjoy suburban lawns and bigger houses. As powell (2000) documents, a series of federal and local policies, including early restrictions in Federal Housing Administration (FHA) loans, the insistence on large public housing projects, and local zoning laws and restrictive covenants, helped struc-ture those choices. After the Fair Housing Act of 1968, new housing frontiers were opened, and both African Ameri-cans and Latinos have been slowly joining the ranks of sub-urban America (see Figure 3-16).

Still, as the figure also shows, there remains a dramatic difference between the percentage of whites and the per-centage of blacks and Latinos who live in suburbs versus central cities. Moreover, some of the outward movement has been to the older and often run-down "inner ring" suburbs

**FIGURE 3-16. Suburbanization of the Population
in Seventy-four Metro Areas, 1970–1990**

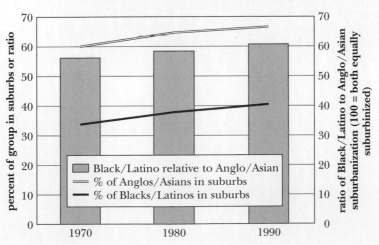

immediately surrounding central cities, and these communities are frequently as fiscally and socially stressed as their central-city neighbors (Orfield, 1997). Nonetheless, the image of the lily-white suburb is giving way to a more multi-hued environment.[6]

However, those left behind in high-poverty areas find their problems exacerbated in several different ways. Figure 3-17, for example, illustrates the suburbanization of employment as jobs have been moving faster than people to the outlying reaches of America's metropolitan regions.

With central cities becoming even more isolated from the economic mainstream, the ratio of central-city poverty to suburban poverty has been rising consistently over the past several decades (see Figure 3-18).

Segregation and concentration also contribute to limited social networks. Despite the proliferation of job placement agencies and temporary employment firms, most job seek-

FIGURE 3-17. Suburbanization of Employment and Population in Seventy-four Metro Areas, 1970–1990

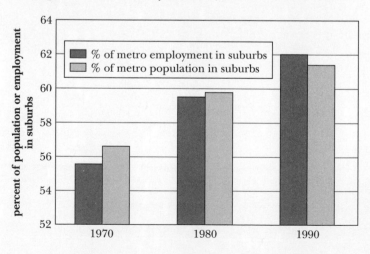

**FIGURE 3-18. Ratio of Central-City to Metro Poverty
in Seventy-four Metro Areas, 1970–1990**

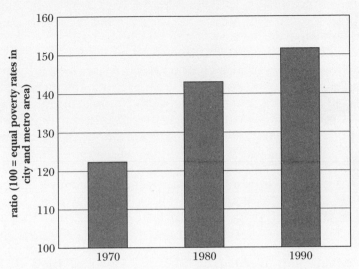

ers still obtain employment through friends, neighbors,
and acquaintances. In areas of concentrated poverty, social
networks are often constrained to those in the immediate
vicinity—and their connections with the job markets are
not the best. As a result, finding good jobs is difficult for
many inner-city residents (see Johnson et al., 2000, and
Pastor and Marcelli, 2001). Loury (1998) notes how neighborhood networks may also play a role in the formation of
norms and expectations about employment, although he
too stresses the straightforward way in which job connections matter. In his words, "Opportunity travels along the
synapses of these social networks." Indeed, the lack of networks in inner-city communities is one way that inequality
is reproduced over time, even when conscious discrimination may not be occurring.

While concentrated poverty has a sharp impact on networks, it contributes to other problems as well, such as
higher crime rates, substandard housing, a lack of role

models, and inadequate schools. Since the white poor are more geographically dispersed, these negative effects of concentration disproportionately affect people of color (Jargowsky, 1997). As a result, any approach to reducing racial disparities must take geography into account. The emerging movement around reducing sprawl and instituting "smart growth" has great potential in this regard.

Education, skills, geographic separation, and social networks—the changing nature of the new economy—has made all of these factors more important. In our high-tech world, skill commands a higher premium; with suburbanized employment, spatial distance can matter more; in a highly networked business world, connections matter increasingly. Internationalization has contributed to the process as well. Competition with lower-wage and lower-skill areas in the rest of the world means that the solid working-class and unionized jobs of an earlier industrial era, often seen as the stepping stones to individual minority economic improvement, have eroded. Unless all these challenges are addressed, there is a potential that the slight progress in closing gaps over the past few years, driven mostly by economic growth, will be overtaken by more fundamental factors. To avoid a widening divide, new ideas and new policies are needed.

Conclusion: Focusing on the Economic

When Bill Clinton ran for president in 1992, his advisors posted a saying in their "war room" that was intended to keep the campaign on point and in focus: "It's the economy, stupid." What was meant then was simple: stressing the need for economic advancement was likely to engender the most voter interest in a tight election.

This focus on the economy can be a very limited—and limiting—view. It is not enough to struggle for material equality. Working on improving human relations is essential for reducing the stereotyping that reduces Asians to foreign "others," renders black and Latino teens special targets of police harassment, and transforms derogatory terms for Native Americans into accepted names for sports teams. Challenging these perspectives is a worthy battle; it is one that will have real consequences, particularly to the extent that negative images in the media and elsewhere influence teachers' perceptions of students and employers' perceptions of workers.

Yet simply reducing prejudice is not enough. A more diverse America is a positive outcome; a more just America would be even better. Achieving equity will require material as well as psychological progress. To do so, America needs both an honest examination of what has been tried in the past and an identification of the issues that will confront it in the future. We turn to these tasks in the next two chapters.

Notes

[1] Both Figure 3-1 and Figure 3-6 offer separate series for whites and non-Latino whites. As noted in the text, the Census Bureau did not distinguish Latinos until the early 1970s, and so we offer the series for all whites (which includes many individuals of Latin American origins) so that we can see the distinctions between black and white income (and poverty in Figure 3-6) over the longer haul. Where the two series cover the same period, we can see a growing distinction between white and non-Latino white income through the 1990s. This itself reflects the growing presence of Latinos, who are generally poorer—and also suggests the caution that should be taken when looking at figures for white income or poverty rates.

[2] While 1.8 percent of all businesses exported in 1992, 2.3 percent of Asian firms and 2.5 percent of Latino firms were involved in exports.

[3] The data in this section are from *Minorities in Business*, 1999, Office of Advocacy, U.S. Small Business Administration, Washington, DC (see www.sba.gov/ADVO/), and the 1997 Economic Census, Minority- and Women-Owned Business, United States (www.census.gov/epcd/mwb97/us/us.html).

[4] See Todd Datz, "Equity," *CIO Magazine*, January 15, 2000; see www.cio.com/archive/011500_equity_content.html.

[5] For more on paired tests, see Fix and Turner (1999). A recent study by the Urban Institute using paired tests found that minorities received less information about loan products and were more likely to be offered higher rates (Turner and Skidmore, 1999).

[6] The data used to calculate the city and suburb population by race come from "The State of the Nation's Cities (SNC), a database that includes information on seventy-four of the country's largest cities and metro areas, with most variables drawn from the 1970, 1980, and 1990 censuses. SNC was compiled by Norman J. Glickman, Michael Lahr, and Elvin Wyly; it was initially assembled under HUD contract by the Center for Urban Policy Research to meet the data needs of the United Nations' Habitat II conference held in Istanbul in June 1996 and has been expanded in variable coverage since. We specifically used version 2.11A (September 22, 1997).

Census 2000 data reinforce the "coloring" of the suburbs. University of Albany (GA) sociologist John Logan, who analyzed suburbs in 330 metropolitan areas, suggests that immigrants are moving to the suburbs "as their first step when they arrive in the country. It used to be you go to the city and then the suburbs" (Nasser, 2001).

References

Association of Community Organizations for Reform Now (ACORN). 2000. *Home Equity and Inequity: An Analysis of Racial and Economic Disparities in Home Purchase Mortgage Lending in Fifty Metropolitan Areas*. Washington, DC: ACORN.

Boston, Thomas D. 2001. "Trends in Minority-Owned Businesses." In Smelser, Neil J., William Julius Wilson, and Faith Mitchell, eds. *Becoming America: Racial Trends and Their Consequences*, Vol. 2. Washington, DC: National Academy Press.

Cavalluzo, Ken, and Linda Cavalluzo. 1998. "Market Structure and Discrimination: The Case of Small Businesses." *Journal of Money, Credit, and Banking*, Vol. 30, No. 4.

Conley, Dalton. 1999. *Being Black, Living in the Red: Race, Wealth, and Social Policy in America*. Berkeley, CA: University of California Press.

Fix, Michael, and Margery Austin Turner, eds. 1999. "A National Report Card on Discrimination in America: The Role of Testing." Washington, DC: The Urban Institute.

Hayes-Bautista, David E. 1993. "Mexicans in Southern California: Societal Enrichment or Wasted Opportunity?" In Abraham F. Lowenthal and Katrina Burgess, eds. *The California-Mexico Connection*. Stanford, CA: Stanford University Press.

Jargowsky, Paul. 1997. *Poverty and Place: Ghettos, Barrios, and the American City*. New York: Russell Sage Foundation.

Johnson, Jr., James H., Elisa Jayne Bienenstock, Walter C. Farrell, Jr., and Jennifer L. Glanville. 2000. "Bridging Social Networks and Female Labor Force Participation in a Multiethnic Metropolis." In Lawrence D. Bobo, Melvin L. Oliver, James H. Johnson, Jr., and Abel Valenzuela, Jr., eds. *Prismatic Metropolis: Inequality in Los Angeles*. New York: Russell Sage Foundation.

Loury, Glenn C. 1998. "Discrimination in the Post-Civil Rights Era: Beyond Market Interactions." *Journal of Economic Perspectives*, Vol. 12, No. 2.

Massey, Douglas S., and Nancy A. Denton. 1993. *American Apartheid: Segregation and the Making of the Underclass*. Cambridge, MA: Harvard University Press.

Moss, Philip, and Chris Tilly. 2001. *Stories Employers Tell: Race, Skill, and Hiring in America*. New York: Russell Sage Foundation.

Nasser, Haya El. 2001. "Minorities Reshape Suburbs." *USA Today*, July 9.

Oliver, Melvin, and Tom Shapiro. 1995. *Black Wealth, White Wealth: A New Perspective on Racial Inequality*. New York: Routledge.

Orfield, Myron. 1997. *Metropolitics: A Regional Agenda for Community and Stability*. Washington, DC: Brookings Institution Press.

Pastor, Jr., Manuel, and Enrico Marcelli. 2001. "Men 'N the Hood: Spatial, Skill, and Social Mismatch for Male Workers in Los Angeles." *Urban Geography*. Forthcoming.

Porter, Michael E. 1995. "The Competitive Advantage of the Inner City." *Harvard Business Review*. May/June.

powell, john a. 2000. "Addressing Regional Dilemmas for Minority Communities." In Bruce Katz, ed. *Reflections on Regionalism*. Washington, DC: Brookings Institution Press.

Turner, Margery Austin, and Felicity Skidmore, eds. 1999. "Mortgage Lending Discrimination: A Review of Existing Evidence." Washington, DC: The Urban Institute.

Yago, Glenn, and Aaron Pankrantz. 2000. *The Minority Business Challenge: Democratizing Capital for Emerging Domestic Markets*. Santa Monica, CA: The Milken Institute.

4

What Works

Fortunately, if America really wants to solve the problem of racial and ethnic inequality, it has a history of programs, strategies, and policies to build upon. Some of these have been race specific—a particularist approach—while others have been more universal in design, tailored to address inequality across racial groups. Regardless of approach, these programs, strategies, and policies have contributed greatly to the advancement of poor people of color in the United States.

This chapter seeks to capture the lessons learned about what it takes to achieve racial justice. It lifts from the many programs the underlying principles that inform the work of achieving racial equality. These principles—based on rights, government policies, community initiatives, wealth building, and participation—represent a particular grid of strategies that enables low-income individuals of color to take responsibility for moving toward and maintaining self-sufficiency. The chapter gives specific examples of how these principles are played out in programs and strategies.

Responses to the problem of inequality over the years

have been varied, ranging from welfare programs that provide a safety net for those most in need to inner-city revitalization strategies that focus on economic development. By lifting up the principles that make a difference in the pursuit of racial justice, this chapter seeks to debunk the myth that nothing works.

The following principles are identified:

- All Americans must have their rights secured and enforced
- Federal policy must set the floor and the framework for achieving equity
- Strategies must be integrated and informed at the community level
- Accumulation of wealth and assets is an important antipoverty strategy
- Voice, participation, and agency are critical for well-being

All Americans Must Have Their Rights Secured and Enforced

The Declaration of Independence, the founding bedrock of American democracy, states that all Americans are entitled to "certain unalienable rights, that among these are life, liberty and the pursuit of happiness." Rights are the centerpiece of American democracy through which opportunity and advancement are achieved. When rights are denied, as they have been to many people over the course of this country's history, including many people of color, inequity results.

Blacks and the Civil Rights Movement

A remarkable testament to human courage, faith, and dignity, the civil rights movement of the 1950s and 1960s showed how much ground can be gained when full rights are secured. In the years preceding the civil rights movement, most African Americans were trapped in dire circumstances with limited rights. For example, "On the eve of World War II, blacks were concentrated in a very confined range of low-paying jobs," with 75 percent of employed black men in 1940 working as farm laborers or machine operators. The black unemployment rate that year was generally 50 to 60 percent higher than that for white Americans (Jaynes and Williams, 1989). As the movement expanded, only 3 percent of black Americans had completed college by 1960 (Hochschild, 1995).

Through protest, mobilization, and litigation, the civil rights movement, while targeted at improving the condition of African Americans, made the country better for everyone. Other groups—Mexican Americans, Puerto Ricans, Native Americans, women—envisioned their issues within the framework of the civil rights struggle and pressed their own claims for justice.

Starting with *Brown v. Board of Education*, the landmark Supreme Court decision that in 1954 declared racial segregation in public schools unconstitutional, the movement gained steam, backed by organizations such as the Southern Christian Leadership Conference (SCLC), the NAACP, the NAACP Legal Defense and Educational Fund, the Congress of Racial Equality (CORE), the Student Nonviolent Coordinating Committee (SNCC), the AFL-CIO, and the National Urban League.

Ten years after *Brown*, Congress passed the Civil Rights Act, outlawing discrimination in employment and racial discrimination in public places—theaters, restaurants, and hotels. Responding to pressure from the civil rights movement and the changing mood in America, President Lyndon B. Johnson signed the Voting Rights Act into law in 1965. The act sought to protect broadly the right of all Americans, including African Americans, to vote, suspending literacy tests and other barriers to enfranchisement while strengthening the federal government's role in overseeing voter registration and elections. President Johnson also signed the Fair Housing Act of 1968, prohibiting dis-

crimination in housing. While this act was criticized for
lacking strong enforcement, it did result in some movement of African Americans and other minorities out of
heavily black inner-city areas into more integrated housing
in surrounding urban and suburban communities.

Without doubt, the civil rights movement transformed
black American life. The black poverty rate declined from
55 percent in 1959 to 32 percent in 1969 (Lemann, 1991).
Affirmative action policies contributed to a growing black
middle class. In 1990, 20 percent of blacks were employed
as managers or professionals, up from 5 percent in 1950. At
the same time, the proportion of African Americans earning more than $50,000 per year more than doubled, from
5.8 percent in 1967 to 13 percent in 1992 (Hochschild,
1995). (The impact of affirmative action is discussed in
more detail later in this chapter.) Between 1967 and 1974,
the percentage of African American high school graduates
grew from 55.9 percent to 67.1 percent, and the number of
African Americans enrolled in college nearly doubled from
297,000 to 555,000, as extrapolated from Table A-5, U.S.
Census Bureau. Homeownership rates of African Americans increased from 34.5 percent in 1950 to 41.6 percent in
1970, as extrapolated from the Historical Census of Housing Tables Ownership Rates, U.S. Census Bureau.

With voting rights officially secured, registration of
African Americans significantly increased. In 1964, approximately 57 percent of eligible blacks remained unregistered
to vote "throughout the former Confederate states" (Lawson, 2000), with the figure in Alabama as high as 77 percent; but within four years, impressive gains were achieved.
By 1968, approximately three-fifths of southern black
Americans had registered to vote. In Mississippi, the registration of black voters soared almost tenfold, from 6.7 percent in 1964 to 59.4 percent. In Alabama, enrollment of
black voters more than doubled, from 23 percent to 53 percent (Lawson, 2000).

The Voting Rights Act transformed the political landscape as well. Between 1965 and 1985, the number of black

representatives in Congress increased from ten to twenty-two; the total number of black elected officials nationwide skyrocketed from 280 in 1965 to 6,829 in 1988 (Jaynes and Williams, 1989). The gains achieved by the civil rights movement continue: the 2000 presidential election saw about 1 million more black votes cast than in 1996, according to the Joint Center for Political and Economic Studies.

Rights for All

The civil rights movement—a race-specific strategy—helped to reverse the plight of African Americans. This particularistic approach has also worked for other marginalized minority groups.

The Chicano movement for justice in the 1960s and 1970s, for instance, gave voice to the frustrations of Mexican Americans. In the 1960s, Mexican Americans were the second largest minority group, numbering 4 to 5 million. Many lived in the Southwest on land that was formerly part of Mexico but was lost at the end of the Mexican-American War. They faced disparate treatment—job and housing discrimination, racial segregation, and social exclusion. Their voting rights were violated, most egregiously in Texas: they were harassed at voting booths, confronted and confounded by poll taxes and English language ballots. "Mexicans were excluded from political participation almost as effectively as Blacks in Mississippi" (Gomez-Quinones, 1990). In 1957, three years after *Brown v. Board of Education*, the *Hernandez et al. v. Driscoll Consolidated Independent School District et al.* case in the U.S. District Court of the Southern District of Texas "brought an end to the practice of requiring Mexican children to spend two years in the first grade" (Gomez-Quinones, 1990).

The Chicano movement shone a national spotlight on issues of culture and language, land and labor, and gave birth to civil rights organizations focused on Latino issues, such as the National Council of La Raza, the Mexican American Legal Defense and Education Fund (MALDEF), the Southwest Voter Registration and Education Project (SWVREP), and the National Association of Latino Elected and Appointed Officials (NALEO). Other civil rights organizations, such as the Puerto Rican Legal Defense and Education Fund, also emerged to safeguard the rights of Latino groups.

These groups were in some ways fashioned after black civil rights organizations, such as the NAACP and the NAACP Legal Defense and Educational Fund. In fact, MALDEF was established in 1967 with the help of the NAACP Legal Defense and Educational Fund.

Over the years, voting rights have also emerged as a key issue for Latinos. MALDEF and SWVREP were instrumental in extending provisions of the Voting Rights Act of 1965 and 1970 to the Chicano community. When Congress was debating extensions to the act in 1975, Latino leaders were sought out for the first time for their views on voting rights issues in their communities. MALDEF and SWVREP strongly backed the extensions to the act, which mandated bilingual election materials in certain jurisdictions with sizable single-language minorities. Latinos have benefited from these efforts, with NALEO reporting significant jumps in the number of Latino elected officials, as chapter 2 noted. MALDEF, known for its effective litigating strategies, also represents the Latino community on cases involving affirmative action and redistricting.

Asian Americans, a group that has been historically victimized, also saw the need for civil rights organizations that would protect their rights and improve the condition of group members. Among the earliest organizations launched were the New York based Asian American Legal Defense and Education Fund (AALDEF), the San Francisco based Asian Law Caucus, and the Los Angeles based Asian Pacific American Legal Center (APALC), the last of which was founded by Stewart Kwoh in 1983. These three groups all effectively litigate on behalf of the rights of Asian Americans. In 1993, APALC, AALDEF, and the Asian Law Caucus founded the National Asian Pacific American Legal Consor-

tium (NAPALC), a Washington, DC based organization that
seeks to advance the legal and civil rights of Asian Americans, litigating on issues such as voting rights and affirmative action.

In the struggle for civil rights, African Americans, Latinos,
Asian Americans, and Native Americans face many similar
challenges. An official coalition of civil rights groups—the
Leadership Conference on Civil Rights (LCCR)—also
emerged as an outgrowth of the civil rights period and exists
to bring greater voice to the pursuit of equity for all marginalized groups in America.

The impact of the black civil rights movement and other
movements that emerged to secure rights for people of
color clearly underscores the importance of securing rights
as a key principle in achieving racial justice.

Federal Policy Must Set the Floor and the Framework for Achieving Equity

The next underlying principle that this chapter lifts up is
the role of the federal government, which must lead by
example and set a universal standard for justice and fairness through its policies. Over the years, federal policies—
both universal and particular—have helped to reduce
inequality within communities of color. Programs designed
to help all groups, such as Aid to Families with Dependent
Children (AFDC), Social Security, and the Earned Income
Tax Credit (EITC), take a universal approach, while affirmative action is an example of a race-specific, particular
approach.

The Universal Approach

Government programs with a universal appeal have had
tremendous impact on reducing inequality overall, including in communities of color. In terms of impact, a study by
the Center on Budget and Policy Priorities, released in
1998, found that government programs such as Social

Security and the Earned Income Tax Credit were instrumental in cutting poverty nearly in half in 1996. Out of 57.5 million people below the poverty line that year, government programs lifted 27 million out of poverty. Moreover, the elderly particularly benefited from safety net programs, with 13 million of them lifted out of poverty. Children also benefited from these programs, though to a lesser degree than the elderly: more than two out of ten would have been poor before receipt of benefits; that rate was nearly cut in half after receipt of benefits (Porter et al., 1998). The particularistic impact of some of these universally designed programs is briefly examined below.

Social Security. While many think of Social Security as a retirement program, it is more than that: it also provides financial support for families in the event of unforeseen circumstances, such as the disability or death of a working or retired parent or spouse. Its survivors' and disability components, in particular, have helped many families of color rise above poverty.

Although African Americans were initially excluded from benefiting from New Deal programs such as Social Security, today they disproportionately receive disability and survivors' benefits from Social Security (Kijakazi, 1998) in part because of the lower life expectancy rate in the African American community. African Americans made up 23 percent of the children and 15 percent of the spouses who received disability benefits in 1996, and they made up 24 percent of the children receiving survivors' benefits.

Studies also show that Social Security is a major source of income for elderly Latinos (Kijakazi, 1998). Twenty-three percent of elderly Latino couples rely on it for all of their income, compared to 9 percent of all elderly couples who receive Social Security.

Earned Income Tax Credit. The Earned Income Tax Credit, enacted in 1975, provides refundable tax credits or wage supplements to working families with children. The EITC has proven more effective at reducing child poverty among working families than any other government program, according to the Center on Budget and Policy Priorities. In 1996, the EITC lifted 4 million people, including 2.4 million children, out of poverty. More than 19 million low- and moderate-income households received the credit that year. The program is particularly effective at reducing poverty in the Latino community because of the high number of Latino families who are classified as working poor (Greenstein and Shapiro, 1998)—a sign of the universal addressing the needs of the particular.

The EITC is an example of a federal program that has been recognized as a model for states to follow. State EITC programs are growing. As of November 2000, fourteen states and the District of Columbia offered their own credit programs, complementing the goals of the federal program by boosting the incomes of families that move from welfare to work and relieving the state and local tax burden borne by low-income families.

Head Start. Head Start, a child development program that provides low-income children with pre-kindergarten experiences, has helped to prepare many children of color for success in school by building their confidence and skills. More than 18 million children have benefited from Head Start, over 800,000 in 1999 alone (U.S. Department of Health and Human Services, 2000). Studies have shown that children from low-income families who participate in early childhood education programs such as Head Start are more likely to succeed in and graduate from school than children from other low-income families who do not participate (see Barnett, 1995; Steinberg, 2001). In 1999, Head Start helped a range of children from all ethnic backgrounds: 30.5 percent of Head Start children were white, 35.1 percent were black, 27.8 percent were Latino, 3.4 percent were Native American, and 3.1 percent were Asian or Pacific Islander (U.S. Department of Health and Human Services, 2000).

Temporary Assistance to Needy Families. Aid to Families with Dependent Children (AFDC) was the cornerstone of America's welfare program until the passage of welfare reform in 1996 creating the Temporary Assistance to Needy Families (TANF) program. At its peak in 1994, AFDC served over 5 million families each month. In 1996, white families made up 35.9 percent of AFDC cases, African American families 37.2 percent, Latino families 20.7 percent, Asian families 3 percent, and Native American families 1.3 percent, with the racial composition of the remainder of the cases registered as unknown (U.S. Department of Health and Human Services, 1998).

TANF, implemented in response to a growing public outcry over the size of the welfare rolls, imposed work requirements and time limits on welfare recipients. It also reduced the government's role in setting a uniform level of benefits, giving more flexibility to states.

TANF has stirred a debate about the appropriate role of the federal government in maintaining safety net benefits while providing a path out of poverty toward self-sufficiency. While some have hailed TANF as a stunning success with welfare rolls cut in half, others contend the program has exacerbated poverty.

Peter Edelman, who reminds his readers in *Searching for America's Heart* that providing for those in need is a concept dating back to the Bible and before, maintains that about 40 percent of the adults no longer on welfare are jobless—a breakout of nearly 1 million people. No one knows what has happened to these adults and their children who number about 3 million. In addition, the poorest 10 percent of single mothers "lost more in welfare and food stamps than they gained in earnings." What's more, many former welfare recipients who get jobs do not escape poverty. "In 1998 the number of family heads with full-time jobs who could not get their families out of poverty was the highest it had been in the twenty-four years that this statistic has been recorded" (Edelman, 2001). Moreover, some are concerned that while caseloads have fallen dramatically, child poverty has not. Welfare rolls dropped nationally by nearly 50 percent between 1993 and 1998, but child poverty dropped by just 17 percent (Sengupta, 2001).

A well-designed safety net program should help to effectively improve the conditions of poor people. As Congress prepares to reauthorize the 1996 welfare reform bill, a closer look must be taken at the weaknesses of TANF with some consideration given to a rethinking of its principles and goals.

The Particular Approach

Affirmative Action. At the same time that the safety net is being weakened, affirmative action programs, which primarily target minorities, are being cut back. The very strategies that have helped to reduce inequality are now being eroded as public opinion has turned against them.

While many think of affirmative action as an outgrowth of the modern civil rights movement, Andrew Hacker maintains that it actually harks back to 1941, "when President Franklin D. Roosevelt signed an Executive Order ordering defense plants to show that they were opening jobs to black workers" (Hacker, 1992). The actual term "affirmative action" was coined by the Kennedy administration, but it was under the Johnson administration that the policy took root.

Affirmative action was designed to correct the injustice of discrimination that many African Americans faced in gaining access to employment and higher education. It acknowledged that the history of slavery and ingrained racism had diminished life chances for many African Americans and excluded them from broad opportunities. Affirmative action was a restorative step premised on showing outcomes. Although affirmative action started out as a program to benefit African Americans, it was expanded to encompass other groups that suffer from discrimination, such as Latinos and Asian Americans, as well as women.

Affirmative action is based upon the principle of equity

or fairness. Latinos, African Americans, Asians, and Native Americans have not received the same types of opportunities as white Americans. As chapter 3 points out, white Americans still dominate the top echelons of corporate America. The equity principle mandates that a particularistic approach be implemented to correct this imbalance by giving more aid to hindered groups.

Despite the controversy surrounding it, affirmative action has been instrumental in breaking down barriers for millions of Americans, affording them access to America's most select universities—"the gateways to prominence, privilege, wealth, and power in American society" (Glazer, 1998)—quality jobs, and business opportunities in contracting. Affirmative action has also opened doors for whites previously excluded by virtue of class and lack of access.

Evidence exists of affirmative action's positive impact. In 1965, the percentage of African Americans enrolled in law school or medical school hovered between 1 and 2 percent, respectively. Many blacks were enrolled in all-black schools. With the Johnson administration's strong commitment to affirmative action, the numbers began to climb. The percentage of black students enrolled in Ivy League colleges rose from 2.3 percent in 1967 to 6.3 percent in 1976. The proportion of black medical students in 1975 stood at 6.3 percent, while the percentage of law students increased to 4.5 percent. By 1995, those numbers had risen, to 8.1 percent and 7.5 percent, respectively (Bowen and Bok, 1998).

The National Asian Pacific American Legal Consortium credits affirmative action with helping to improve education and employment opportunities for many Asian Americans. NAPALC cites a study showing that with affirmative action 26 percent of Asian Americans who applied to accredited law schools in the fall of 1991 were admitted; without affirmative action, the study showed that only 15 percent of the Asian American students would have been admitted (National Asian Pacific American Legal Consortium, 1998). At the same time, since the inception of California's civil service affirmative action program in 1977, Asian Americans achieved labor force parity in eleven out of nineteen state job categories (National Asian Pacific American Legal Consortium, 1998). Moreover, the participation of Asian Americans in San Francisco's Unified School District construction contracts tripled to 17.35 percent in 1993 after the district implemented an affirmative action program (National Asian Pacific American Legal Consortium, 1998).

Although affirmative action has had a proven track record in reducing inequality, it has come under fire for allegedly promoting "preferences"; its future is unclear. Recent court battles have chipped away at its legitimacy: the *Hopwood v. State of Texas* case in 1995 ended affirmative action in Texas's state university system; in March 2001, a federal judge ruled that the race-conscious admissions policy of the University of Michigan's law school was unconstitutional; and the Supreme Court—in a series of cases—has tightened the standards that federal affirmative action programs must meet, and is once more set to hear yet another case in the fall of 2001 that challenges the constitutionality of affirmative action in contracting.[1]

State challenges have also surfaced, most prominently with Proposition 209 in California, which outlawed affirmative action in public employment, public education, and public contracting in 1996. Five years after Proposition 209's "victory," the numbers of African Americans admitted to the state's two most prestigious campuses in the university system—Berkeley and Los Angeles—"remain more than 40 percent lower than in 1997" (Trounson and Weiss, 2001). While new equity based formulations are emerging as an alternative to affirmative action in a few higher education systems across the country (see Box 4-1), it remains to be seen whether they represent a broad based trend. It cannot be stated more emphatically: affirmative action–type programs are needed to achieve equity in America.

The federal government must take the lead in imple-

Box 4-1. Beyond Affirmative Action: New Lessons in Equity

In an era of increasing diversity, affirmative action has become highly controversial as a policy that promotes "reverse discrimination." Some also say it results in the hiring and selection of unqualified people for jobs and college. Studies have shown that white Americans, in particular, are opposed to affirmative action. In 1990, almost 70 percent of white Americans said they opposed quotas to admit black students to colleges and universities, and more than 80 percent objected to the idea of preferential hiring and promotion of African Americans (Wilson, 1999).

Affirmative action has a proven track record of achieving equity and inclusion in America. The future of the country depends on a policy that continues to groom and develop a diverse cadre of individuals for leadership. Polls show that many African Americans are as strong in their support of affirmative action as white Americans are opposed. How is this situation to be resolved?

The future may lie in innovative formulations that are emerging, grounded in the principle of equity.

These new formulations are being tested in Texas, Florida, and California, after those states banned affirmative action in education. The strategies, all variations on a theme, appear to be working.

Black and Latino state legislators in Texas, concerned about maintaining a certain level of minority enrollment in the state university after affirmative action was banned, conceived of a plan that would guarantee continued representation of minority groups. Texas's plan grants automatic admission to state colleges to all students graduating in the top 10 percent of their high school classes. Close observers say the plan has been "remarkably successful" (Guinier, 2000). Not only have poor white counties in rural Texas sent graduates to the flagship state university in Austin for the first time, but African American freshman enrollment increased 50 percent over the year immediately after the *Hopwood* decision. The number of Latino students has also increased "to more than when affirmative action was the official policy" (Guinier, 2000). Fears that the students who got in under the 10 percent plan would not meet academic expectations did not materialize. The collective grade point average of the students in their first year of college was "higher than the freshman average for all students before the *Hopwood* decision" (Guinier, 2000).

California and Florida have implemented similar plans. At the University of California, where the number of black, Latino, and Native American students plummeted following the decision to abolish affirmative action, a plan has been proposed to "guarantee provisional admission to the top 12.5 percent of students at every high school" (Arenson, 2000), complementing an existing plan that guarantees admission to the top 12.5 percent of students statewide. It is expected that the new plan would attract about 12,000 additional students, more than a third of whom would be black, Latino, or Native American. The earliest students would be enrolled under this plan is September 2002, although it may be as late as 2003. To reach a more diverse base of students, California also started a program last year offering admission to the top 4 percent of the students at each high school in the state.

In Florida, Governor Jeb Bush put an end to race based admissions and introduced a plan that allows admission of the top 20 percent of graduating seniors from each state high school, whether predominantly black, white, or Latino, to Florida's state college system. The first freshman class last year represented an increase in minority enrollment of 12 percent, or, to put it another way, produced an incoming class of more than 40 percent minority (Bragg, 2000). At Florida's flagship state-run universities—the University of Florida and Florida State University—the number of black students enrolled grew 33 percent and 21 percent, respectively, from last year. The number of Latino students grew by 19 percent at the University of Florida and by 24 percent at Florida State.

menting, maintaining, and modeling policies that are fair and equitable, setting an example for state and local policy makers to follow.

Strategies Must Be Integrated and Informed at the Community Level

Ultimately, people live in communities, and one successful approach to reducing inequity in low-income communities of color engages residents in problem solving and addresses their complex needs in an integrated fashion. Known as community building, this approach has emerged over the past fifteen years as a promising framework for sustainable change. Community building shares some of its principles with the War on Poverty, an approach implemented in the 1960s under President Johnson. Like the War on Poverty, community building emphasizes the involvement of residents in addressing their needs and recognizes the complexity of factors that perpetuate inequity.

A key strength of community building is its involving local residents in shaping solutions. Community building brings together broad cross-sections of a community, including residents, corporate leaders, law enforcement officials, schools, and clergy to solve problems that are complex and interconnecting. It promotes the participation of usually excluded people in making decisions that affect their lives, bridging the usual barriers of race and class. Community building strategies are helping to turn around the fortunes of many low-income communities of color. In Oakland, CA, community building helped to reduce infant mortality in targeted areas of the black community by 50 percent and contributed to a drastic reduction in homicides among African American and Latino youths in Boston.

One of the key lessons from the community building field is the need to integrate "people" and "place" strategies, combining strategies focused on health, education, and family support with those addressing housing, retail development, and transportation. The confluence of "people" and "place" strategies yields integrated, comprehensive solutions.

A recent series of articles in the *New York Times* focusing on the transformation of 129th Street in Harlem hinted at the importance of focusing on the needs of people when neighborhoods are being physically improved. One article pointed out, "Amid the transformed buildings and transplanted residents, the way up, or out, for many of the block's residents still seems poorly mapped. Limestone facades can be scrubbed. Limited education, racism, defeatist thinking, addiction, and a shifting economy are harder to overcome" (Waldman, 2001a). A companion article called attention to the fact that it is "easier to transform buildings than lives" (Waldman, 2001b).

New Community Corporation in Newark, NJ, has found a way to transform lives as well as buildings. It is generally regarded as a model of an integrated strategy. Founded a year after the 1967 Newark riots, its mission is to help inner-city residents improve the quality of their lives "to reflect individual dignity and personal achievement" (PolicyLink, 2000). New Community came to prominence in the 1980s and is now the nation's largest community development corporation (CDC) with an annual budget of "more than $100 million and more than fourteen-hundred employees" (Edelman, 2001). New Community offers a wide range of services: housing, day care, an elementary school, and a shopping center anchored by a Pathmark supermarket. In July 1999, it opened its Work-force Development Center as a one-stop career center. The three-story, 25,000-square-foot, state-of-the-art center is slated to serve 2,000 people annually with welfare-to-work and job training programs.

Integrated community building strategies informed by the voice of community residents are providing a new model of the solutions that are possible to inequity. They are yet another part of the equation in the search for racial justice.

Accumulation of Wealth and Assets Is an Important Antipoverty Strategy

Antipoverty strategies for poor people of color have not traditionally focused on building wealth. Yet, wealth building mechanisms have allowed many Americans to accumulate assets and move well beyond poverty. For example, the Federal Housing Administration (FHA) has made it possible for millions of Americans to buy homes, providing a source of equity that financed their children's college education and that started businesses. The federal mortgage deduction remains a source of additional funds for many homeowners. The Small Business Administration has helped entrepreneurs start and sustain their businesses. Attention is now being paid to more deliberate use of wealth building strategies as an approach for reducing poverty.

In 1991, Michael Sherraden and Neil Gilbert, in *Assets and the Poor*, called attention to the need for asset building in poor communities, arguing that welfare policy had failed because the concept of assets had not been considered. Assets are beneficial in complex ways, they maintained, helping to improve household stability; psychologically connect people with a viable, hopeful future; stimulate development of other assets; provide a foundation for risk taking; enhance the welfare of offspring; and increase social influence and political participation.

Melvin Oliver and Thomas Shapiro (1995) echo that need in *Black Wealth/White Wealth*, a detailed look at the wealth disparity between black and white Americans. Noting that it is through wealth, not income, that one provides for the next generation, the authors point out that African Americans have never had the luxury of accumulating wealth to the same extent as white Americans because of their history of slavery and segregation. (For more information on the racial wealth gap, see chapter 3.) Oliver and Shapiro emphasize the need to develop a consciousness in the African American community around wealth building. The growth of minority businesses, as mentioned in chapter 3, is an encouraging route for reducing the wealth gap.

Advocates for low-income communities of color are increasingly incorporating wealth building as a strategy for reducing inequity, looking beyond homeownership to investments in business and real estate. Several organizations, including the Corporation for Enterprise Development (CfED), Fannie Mae, and PolicyLink, are among those spearheading efforts to advance and disseminate these new wealth building tools. As a result, savings, ownership, and investment—concepts not normally associated with the poor—are gaining attention as antipoverty strategies for the 21st century (PolicyLink, 2001).

One evolving strategy is Individual Development Accounts (IDAs) to increase savings in low-income communities. IDAs are matched savings accounts, similar to Individual Retirement Accounts (IRAs). CfED initiated the first nationwide demonstration of IDAs in 1997. In IDAs, participants set up savings accounts at local banks or credit unions, and sponsoring organizations deposit matching funds in separate accounts. IDAs may be used only for specific, preapproved purposes, such as purchasing a home, paying for post-secondary education or training, or starting a small business.

Currently, twenty-nine states and the District of Columbia have passed IDA legislation; more than 250 IDA programs are operating nationwide. In October 1998,

President Clinton signed into law the Assets for Independence Act, a multimillion-dollar initiative that authorized the U.S. Department of Health and Human Services to conduct a five-year, $25-million-per-year IDA demonstration. IDAs were included in the Welfare Reform Act of 1996, allowing states to establish IDA programs using TANF funds. Many states provide direct appropriations for IDA programs, with funds matched directly from the state treasury (PolicyLink, 2001).

Gaming has recently emerged as a strategy for pursuing wealth in some Native American communities. According to the First Nations Development Institute, approximately 188 tribes operate 285 gaming facilities in twenty-eight states. One of the more successful tribes has been the Oneida, based in the Green Bay, WI, metropolitan area. In fiscal year 1995, gaming represented 84.7 percent of the tribe's total income of about $203 million. The Oneidas have been able to diversify economic enterprises on the reservation through activities such as raising beef, maintaining an orchard and a cannery, and operating convenience stores. They also operate a large hotel, restaurant, and conference facility near the casino. With increased income, the tribe has been able to run a variety of social programs for its members, including childcare, alcohol and drug abuse prevention, mental health services, housing, and early childhood development (Alesch, 1997).

Other efforts are emerging to develop and expand new models that have the potential for building resident ownership in real estate and commercial development projects so that low-income communities of color benefit from market trends instead of being displaced by them. In the real estate arena, Real Estate Investment Trusts (REITs) offer a promising model. When REITs were established over thirty years ago, they were aimed at opening opportunities for real estate investment to small investors and diversifying risk to those investors, much like a mutual fund. After regulatory changes in the 1990s, the use of REITs increased dramatically. Recent efforts have transformed REITs into a tool for community development. In 1999, for example, the Community Land Trust based in New York established a REIT for affordable housing and community development purposes (PolicyLink, 2001).

Building on the REIT model and the twin notions of reducing risks and building opportunities for small-scale investors, one effort is looking at opportunities to include low-income residents as investors in community real estate assets. For example, a "community building REIT" could invest in real estate within a community and sell shares of the portfolio to residents as well as to outside investors. Explorations are also underway to increase resident ownership in new and existing businesses in low-income communities. Some of the models being considered are worker co-ops—where workers are also business owners—and Employee Stock Ownership Plans (ESOPs)—where employees are given opportunities to gain equity in the businesses where they work (PolicyLink, 2001).

One model of a cooperative business venture that has attracted the attention of community development experts is in the Columbia Heights neighborhood of Washington, DC. Realizing they lacked a laundromat and sensing an opportunity to advance their neighborhood's economy, residents of this low-income neighborhood drafted a business plan and initiated a public offering to establish such a venture within the neighborhood. Known as B.I.G. Wash, the laundromat opened in 1995, with $30,000 raised among the residents. The laundromat remains a successful business enterprise, with annual revenues of nearly a quarter million dollars, a payroll of about $70,000, employing neighborhood residents as bookkeepers, auditors, and monitors. The equity in and annual dividends from B.I.G. Wash increased the financial stability of the member residents, enabling some of them to purchase their homes (Nembhard, 2000).

Wealth building strategies are an innovative vehicle for bridging the inequality gap in communities of color. They should be recognized as newly emerging tools that can help redirect market forces to the benefit, instead of the detriment, of low-income people.

Voice, Participation, and Agency Are Critical for Well-Being

No strategy for achieving justice works without the voice and participation of racial and ethnic minorities acting as agents of change in their own behalf. Because low-income communities of color have been marginalized and excluded for so long, it has become common for outsiders to make decisions that affect them. But low-income communities should not wait to be acted upon; they have power and the ability to make things happen. These notions of agency, voice, and participation are well demonstrated in community- and labor-organizing efforts. When low-income communities have mobilized, incredible things have happened.

An effort to improve the Zavala Elementary School in East Austin, TX, demonstrates the power of community organizing. Zavala, one of the Alliance Schools of the Texas Industrial Areas Foundation (IAF) network, was struggling in 1991. The percentage of its students passing state mandated achievement tests was about half the district average. Among Austin's sixty-three elementary schools, Zavala ranked thirty-third in school attendance. The students and their parents, many Spanish speaking, were locked into a cycle of low expectations.

Through community organizing, parents, teachers, administrators, public officials, and other community members began changing the destiny of the school and its students. Parents and teachers first partnered to create a health clinic at the school. Shortly thereafter, in September 1993, Zavala opened an after-school program with a broad range of offerings. That same year, the Zavala Young Scientists Program was inaugurated. In 1994, six students from the Young Scientists Program were admitted to the science magnet program at a nearby junior high school—a first in Zavala history. Only one Zavala student had previously been admitted to this program; in 1995, seven were admitted. In the 1993–94 school year, Zavala dramatically ascended from thirty-third in school attendance to a tie for first place; the next school term, it was the clear champion. During these years, Zavala's results in state achievement tests improved, with the percentage of students passing the reading and mathematics tests higher than citywide averages. In a short period of time, Zavala accomplished remarkable results through organizing the school community and promoting the principle of voice.

In Los Angeles, Metropolitan Alliance, a multiracial group, effectively waged a campaign to win benefits for the low-income Latino and African American community, using a public subsidy as leverage. In 1998, a proposed $70 million subsidy was offered to DreamWorks Inc., a new motion picture studio founded by Steven Spielberg, Jeffrey Katzenberg, and David Geffen. Although Hollywood is big business, people of color in general, and working-class people in particular, historically have been locked out. Metropolitan Alliance developed a plan that would link the subsidy proposed for DreamWorks' development to public benefits for Los Angeles's inner-city communities. The aim was to create job training and career development opportunities for low-income residents.

The public campaign convinced DreamWorks to create and provide resources for a Work-force Development Fund that would support multimedia-entertainment training at community colleges for economically disadvantaged residents. In addition, DreamWorks and the developers committed to placing participants from training programs in at least 10 percent of the jobs created through the development project. The alliance officially became a partner with DreamWorks and the city of Los Angeles to develop and monitor these programs. Although DreamWorks decided not to locate on the proposed site, it nevertheless agreed to honor its commitment to the Work-force Development Fund, including providing an initial $5 million to get the programs started—evidence of the power of the campaign.

Other effective alliances are evolving that reinforce the principles of voice and participation. In 1998, the AFL-CIO launched a multiunion effort in Stamford, CT, to organize the city's struggling service-sector workers. The drive was unusual in two respects: it required interunion cooperation and embraced community-organizing goals. The Stamford Organizing Project (SOP) targeted low-wage workers—many African American and Latino—from a variety of sectors and started addressing larger community problems such as affordable housing. The campaign garnered intensive media coverage and "placed the housing crisis at the top of local lawmakers' agendas" (Fine, 2001). It led to the repeal of a pilot housing privatization law and triggered a new legislative deal worth $10 million in affordable housing construction funds. The AFL-CIO also offered up to $50 million in finance capital from its pension funds to match state spending dollar-for-dollar on affordable housing programs.

As a result, unions in Stamford have gained increased respect and have seen a steady rise in their numbers, increasing their bargaining powers: the janitorial union, SEIU, successfully organized 2,700 janitors in the fall of 2000 and negotiated a new contract, raising the hourly wage from the legal minimum of $6.15 to $9. The United Auto Workers has also started organizing childcare, hospital, and assisted living workers, as well as taxi drivers. In such drives, the SOP's community oriented approach has been credited for its successes.

Through community- and labor-organizing activities, poor communities of color have effectively advocated for themselves and brought about incredible change. The examples just provided serve as reminders that strong, organized communities have the power through their voice to improve the situation of poor people of color and chart new destinies.

Conclusion

Much is known about what works to reduce racial inequality: a commitment to rights, fair and equitable government policies, integrated and informed community building strategies, wealth building efforts, and attention to voice and participation. These principles build on and reinforce each other. Rights secure the path to opportunity; government policies ensure that fairness and equity are preserved; community building strategies complement federal efforts at the local level; wealth building activities contribute to local solutions; and paying attention to voice makes all communities vibrant. As America searches for the uncommon common ground, these principles are paramount in facing the new policy challenges that lie ahead.

Note

[1] The 1989 Supreme Court ruling in *City of Richmond v. J.A. Croson* set a higher standard for states and local governments to prove the existence of disparity in government contracting and the need for affirmative action programs. While not striking down the principle, the Supreme Court applied this same level of scrutiny to federal affirmative action programs, with *Adarand Constructors v. Peña* in 1995, extending strict scrutiny beyond contracting. The debate will be renewed in the high court's 2001–2002 term with Adarand Constructors—a contracting company based in Colorado Springs, CO—yet again appealing the constitutionality of affirmative actions programs.

References

Alesch, Daniel J. 1997. "The Impact of Indian Casino Gambling on Metropolitan Green Bay." Thiensville, WI: Wisconsin Policy Research Institute, Inc.

Arenson, Karen W. 2000. "California Proposal Aims to Improve College Diversity." *New York Times*, September 22.

Barnett, W.S. 1995. "Long-term Effects of Early Childhood Programs on Cognitive and School Outcomes." *The Future of Children*, Vol. 5, No. 3.

Bowen, William G., and Derek Bok. 1998. *The Shape of the River.* Princeton, NJ: Princeton University Press.

Bragg, Rick. 2000. "Minority Enrollment Rises in Florida College System." *New York Times*, August 30.

Edelman, Peter. 2001. *Searching for America's Heart: RFK and the Renewal of Hope*. Boston and New York: Houghton Mifflin Company.

Fine, Janice. 2001. "Building Community Unions." *The Nation*, January 1.

Glazer, Nathan. 1998. "In Defense of Preference." *The New Republic*, April 6.

Gomez-Quinones, Juan. 1990. *Chicano Politics*. Albuquerque, NM: University of New Mexico Press.

Greenstein, Robert, and Isaac Shapiro. 1998. *New Research Findings on the Effects of the Earned Income Tax Credit*. Washington, DC: Center on Budget and Policy Priorities, March 11.

Guinier, Lani. 2000. "Credit Bush Doesn't Deserve." *New York Times*, August 1.

Hacker, Andrew. 1992. *Two Nations: Black and White, Separate, Hostile, Unequal*. New York: Charles Scribners' Sons.

Hochschild, Jennifer L. 1995. *Facing Up to the American Dream*. Princeton, NJ: Princeton University Press.

Jaynes, Gerald David, and Robin M. Williams, eds. 1989. *Common Destiny: Blacks and American Society*. Washington, DC: National Academy Press.

Kijakazi, Kilolo. 1998. "African Americans, Hispanic Americans, and Social Security: The Shortcomings of the Heritage Foundation Reports." Washington, DC: Center on Budget and Policy Priorities, October 8.

Lawson, Steven F. 2000. "The Selma Movement and the Voting Rights Act of 1965." In *Civil Rights Since 1787*, Jonathan Birnbaum and Clarence Taylor, eds. New York: New York University Press.

Lemann, Nicholas. 1991. *The Promised Land: The Great Black Migration and How It Changed America*. New York: Alfred Knopf, Inc.

National Asian Pacific American Legal Consortium. 1998. *Speaker's Manual on Affirmative Action*. Washington, DC: National Asian Pacific American Legal Consortium.

Nembhard, Jessica Gordon. 2000. "Entering the New City as Men and Women, Not Mules: Democratic and Humane Economic Development Strategies for Revitalizing Inner Cities." Unpublished Manuscript.

Oliver, Melvin L., and Thomas M. Shapiro. 1995. *Black Wealth/White Wealth: A New Perspective on Racial Inequality*. New York: Routledge.

PolicyLink. 2001. *Sharing the Wealth: Resident Ownership Mechanisms*. Oakland, CA: PolicyLink.

———. 2000. *Communities Now!* Oakland, CA: PolicyLink.

Porter, Kathy, Wendell Primus, Lynette Rawlings, and Esther Rosenbaum. 1998. *Strengths of the Safety Net: How the EITC, Social Security, and*

Other Government Programs Affect Poverty. Washington, DC: Center on Budget and Policy Priorities.

Sengupta, Somini. 2001. "How Many Poor Children Is Too Many?" *New York Times,* July 8.

Sherraden, Michael, and Neil Gilbert. 1991. *Assets and the Poor: A New American Welfare Policy.* Armonk, NY: M.E. Sharpe.

Steinberg, Jacques. 2001. "Gains Found for the Poor in Rigorous Preschool." *New York Times,* May 9.

Trounson, Rebecca, and Kenneth R. Weiss. 2001. "Number of Blacks, Latinos Admitted to UC System Rise." *Los Angeles Times,* April 4.

U.S. Department of Health and Human Services. 2000. *2000 Head Start Statistical Fact Sheet.* www2.acf.dhhs.gov/programs/hsb/research/oo_hsfs.htm.

———. 1998. *Aid to Families with Dependent Children: The Baseline.* http://aspe.hhs.gov/hsp/AFDC/afdcbase98.htm.

Waldman, Amy. 2001(a). "Beneath Harlem Block's New Surface, a Dark Undertow." *New York Times,* February 19.

———. 2001(b). "Embodied by One Block, Harlem's Ravaged Heart Sees a Revival." *New York Times,* February 18.

Wilson, William Julius. 1999. *The Bridge over the Racial Divide: Rising Inequality and Coalition Politics.* Berkeley, CA: University of California Press.

5

New Challenges

As America enters the new millennium, some of the contemporary challenges to racial equality it faces seem to harken back to an earlier era. Formal segregation in schools was struck down long ago, but stark disparities in educational opportunity by race and ethnicity persist, and *de facto* separation by race in the educational system spells isolation in children's daily lives. Employment, housing, and credit discrimination have eased, but "paired tests"—in which black and white candidates with similar backgrounds are sent to apply for jobs, apartments, or loans—suggest that prejudice remains alive. Even racial differences in effective suffrage—a problem thought settled after the elimination of poll taxes, literacy requirements, and the like—have resurfaced as a key issue following the Florida recount in the 2000 presidential elections. Provided with older voting machines and less adequate phone and computer services, voters in heavily minority precincts may have lost the franchise that so many civil rights pioneers struggled hard to secure.

Meanwhile, new and more complex issues have arisen to

cloud the picture for racial equity in America. The digital economy, with the value it places on skills and social networks, is contributing to a widening gap in economic fortunes by class and race. Environmental racism—a pattern by which industrial and other hazards are disproportionately concentrated in minority communities—has arisen as a primary issue for many communities. The disproportionate presence of black and Latino men in the criminal justice system—with some beginning to view prison as an unfortunate rite of passage and others caught up in the "racial profiling" produced by social hysteria and an undisciplined police— has resulted in large parts of a generation losing their right to vote and facing significant barriers to employment.

These issues are both new and old: the digital divide may simply reflect earlier differences in technology access; environmental inequity partly results from the intersection of housing segregation and industrial decline; and the swelling prison population partly signals a failure to provide hope for minority youth. But these issues are also more complex than, say, voting rights, and their racial meaning and character need to be unpacked and examined if the nation is to make progress on achieving racial equality in America.

In this chapter, we highlight some of these new challenges and recommend solutions to them. Some of the solutions reflect the principles of fair and equitable government policies, community oriented approaches, and attention to voice and participation lifted up in the previous chapter.

This chapter focuses on six issues: (1) education, (2) suburban sprawl, (3) environmental justice, (4) the "digital divide," (5) immigrant incorporation, and (6) the criminal justice system. The first four of these issues—education, sprawl, environmental justice, and the changes wrought by the digital economy—raise concerns shared by many Americans, whether whites or persons of color, middle class or poor. Indeed, the political appeal of this set of issues is that they tap into universal interests; at the same time, addressing the problems requires racial specificity in both our analysis and our solutions.

The last two concerns—immigrant policy and the criminal justice system—are often more politically challenging to raise: they initially seem to be more directed at solving problems faced by particular groups. We argue, however, that failure to address these questions will have negative consequences for all Americans—and that the traditional distinction between "universal" and "particularistic" approaches to issue identification and problem solving may therefore be false. This point is so central to our analysis that we begin with it below; the rest of the chapter is taken up by a discussion of the issue areas and potential policy directions for the future.

Universalism, Particularism, and a New Paradigm

Few things may be worse in U.S. politics than being accused of representing "special interests." While the term may conjure up corporate lobbyists and quiet contributors, it has also been applied to minority Americans asking for special programs to correct past wrongs or meet particular needs, such as set-asides for black owned businesses, repayment for assets taken from Japanese Americans interned during World War II, bilingual education for the growing Latino population, or reparations for African Americans. Indeed, the popular discourse has shifted such that particularistic approaches—such as affirmative action strategies to produce a better mix in college and employment pools—have been reframed as "preferences."

Because of this backlash, some authors, such as Harvard sociologist William Julius Wilson (1999), focus on policy packages with broad common ground appeal. In his view, stressing affirmative action or the specific plight of blacks or Latinos in the inner city will alienate voters and other social actors who see little direct connection to their own lives—particularly white working-class people worried about their own livelihoods or their children's college chances in a globalized and highly competitive economy. In contrast, securing government commitments to maintain full employment or better fund public education will help everyone—and therefore reinforce natural coalitions—even as they have especially positive effects on minorities who are frequently the last hired in an economic recovery and whose children often have little choice but public schools.

Such "universalism" certainly has great appeal: after all, the periods of most rapid advancement in minority political rights have come when seemingly "special" demands are wrapped in the language of universal concerns. For example, the civil rights movement may have focused on empowering African Americans, but the call to the basic ideals of the republic, including the rights to speak and vote, and the attraction of a strategy of nonviolent resistance, moved many white Americans to sympathize with the cause and yielded benefits to other minorities as well as to women. The immigration reform law of 1965 may have opened the doors to Latino and Asian newcomers, but its contribution to the extraordinary growth of these populations in recent years was partly due to the reaffirmation of a family reunification principle solidly based in traditional and commonly held American values.

While universalism should be a theme and a goal, one cannot ignore the felt experience of oppression and the clear and ongoing needs of particular populations. Opponents of programs targeted at helping minority Americans may refer longingly to the "color-blind" ideals of the civil rights movement, but the civil rights movement was not oblivious to color: it was exactly the liberation of black Americans from Jim Crow that was at issue. And the contemporary situation—in which the probability of being involved in the criminal justice system is seven times higher for black males than for white males—cries out for "particularistic" analysis and action.

In our view, hard and fast distinctions between universal and particular approaches—and strict preferences for one over the other—are unproductive. What is needed instead is a paradigm that combines a call for the universal common good with attention to the particular experience of minority Americans—what Theda Skocpol (1991) once called "targeting within universalism." The first of the issues we explore—education, sprawl, environmental justice, and the divide in the digital economy—fall exactly along those lines: they offer the possibility of shared goals even as they address entrenched racial disparities. The next two issues, immigrant incorporation and inequities in the criminal justice system, are perhaps more particular: as noted above, their effects are felt most dramatically by U.S. minorities and, as a result, they have engendered a very small constituency of concerned white Americans. Yet they are too central to be left aside, and those concerned about racial equality must work to widen the circle of caring about these issue areas as well.

The Road Ahead:
Key Issues for the 21st Century

Education and Race

Educational reform has become the mantra of nearly every politician, most businesspeople, and virtually all parents—and improving American education would go a long way to relieving some of the economic and social inequities revealed in chapter 3. Of course, not all the news is bad: as Figure 5-1 illustrates, between 1970 and 2000, the high school completion gap between white and black Americans closed considerably.

The Latino population has made significantly less progress, with high school completion rates still below the 60 percent level.[1]

While a high school education means less in today's technologically driven economy, one cannot overlook that it feeds the college pipeline. In terms of college completion

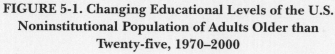

FIGURE 5-1. Changing Educational Levels of the U.S.
Noninstitutional Population of Adults Older than
Twenty-five, 1970–2000

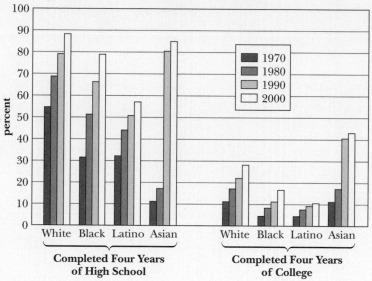

rates, black Americans have made some progress, but the
improvement has not been as dramatic as the gains in high
school completion. The rate of Latino improvement on college completion measures has been very limited, with
hardly any gains in the 1990s. The Asian educational level
is actually extraordinarily high; while this partly reflects the
arrival of highly educated Asian immigrants, U.S.-born
Asians have also achieved great success in education.

These differences in education make a big difference in
economic outcomes: Figure 5-2 shows earnings by educational category for white Americans, African Americans,
and Latinos (figures were unavailable at a similar level of
detail for Asians and other groups).

As can be seen, earnings rise with education for all
groups. For blacks and Latinos, there is a substantial earn-

FIGURE 5-2. Earnings by Race by Educational Category, Average 1998–1999

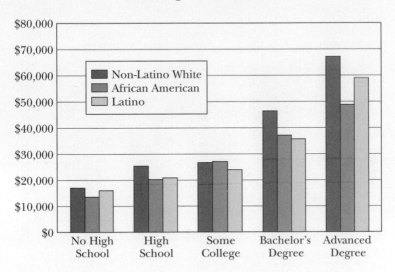

ings improvement between having a high school education and having some years of college—indeed, there is near parity across the racial groups for the latter category—suggesting the potential importance of community colleges to minority Americans. There is also a dramatic income gain from going to college, a fact that explains why affirmative action for higher educational institutions has been such a priority for minority leaders.

Note, however, that earnings disparities by race persist at every educational level, suggesting that education alone will not erase the effects of spatial mismatch, discrimination, and other factors. There are, for example, wide gaps between white and minority Americans even when both have bachelor's degrees; while some of this may reflect age (since black Americans and Latinos have more recently gained entrance in larger numbers to universities, the resulting adult population is younger and earlier in their

FIGURE 5-3. Composition of Elementary, High School, and College Enrollment in the United States by Race and Latino Origin, 1998

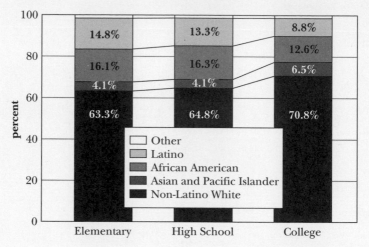

lifetime earnings profile), it also seems to be a function of the different social networks enjoyed by white and minority graduates.

Will the situation improve in the future as more students of color move through an improved pipeline and swell the ranks of young adults with a college education? Figure 5-3 shows the composition of the contemporary elementary, high school, and college student bodies; as can be seen, there is a precipitous drop-off for African Americans and Latinos as we move from high school to college.

Education is also not just a matter of completing years: there is a significant gap in performance at different steps in the process. Figure 5-4 offers a look at one measure, average reading proficiency scores by age and ethnicity for the period 1980–1999.

The gaps in scores are large at all levels, and while there seems to be some improvement for African Americans and Latinos in the seventeen-year-old group, this may simply

**FIGURE 5-4. U.S. Average Reading Proficiency Scale
Scores, 1980 through 1999 Long-Term Trend Summary
Chart for Ages Nine, Thirteen, and Seventeen**

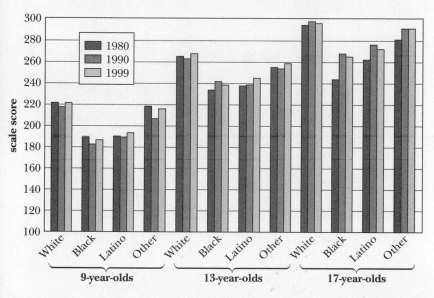

reflect rising dropout rates and thus a rise in the selectivity
of those taking the test.[2]

Christopher Jencks and Meredith Phillips (1998) have
written that "if racial equality is America's goal, reducing
the black-white test score gap would probably do more to
promote this goal than any other strategy that could
command broad political support." A new spate of
research suggests that some of the difference in performance on standardized tests may have to do with "stereotype anxiety"—students believing that by virtue of their
membership in a particular group they are not expected
to do well. Claude Steele of Stanford University, for
example, has found that minority students who are asked
to list their race before taking an exam do worse than
those who do not—he suggests that the request for self-

identification leads to a buy-in of societal doubts about their performance.[3]

What should be done? Clearly, a key issue is the racial divide in school quality, with a disproportionate number of minority youngsters confined to poorly performing inner-city schools. While many Americans say that they favor the school integration that was once viewed as key to minority success (see Figure 5-5),[4] integration has become increasingly less popular as a strategy: as indicated in Figure 5-6, there has been a dramatic swing in those who favor improving funding to minority schools over integration efforts.

While this may reflect a quiet desire for separation, it also seems that many Americans have come to believe that shifting attitudes will not necessarily yield material progress and that direct investments in the educational institutions where underperformance is a problem might be more useful for promoting racial equality.

The new consensus around targeting resources to

FIGURE 5-5. Attitudes Toward School Integration, 1988–1999

Do you believe that more should be done or that less should be done to integrate schools throughout the nation?

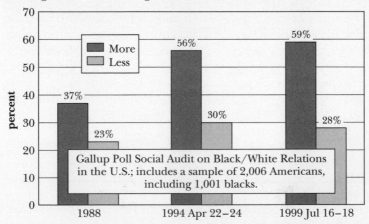

FIGURE 5-6. Increasing Integration versus Increasing Funding

Which do you think is the better way to help minority students, step up efforts to integrate or increase funding and other resources?

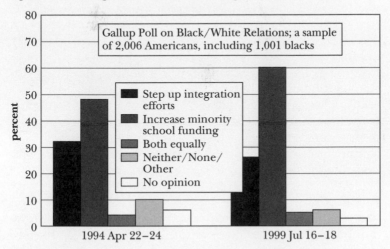

minority youngsters is increasingly bipartisan. President Bush's educational program focuses on the poorest and lowest-performing schools, a concern shared by Democratic leaders and many educational experts. Of course, there remain significant differences about the best way to get there—the relative size of the investment, the proper role for testing standards, and the extent to which public policy should support enhanced parental choice via vouchers. Still, that there is a widespread sentiment for targeted action is encouraging.

At the university level, debate continues about the proper role of affirmative action, as we spell out in chapter 4. In California, where voters eliminated the explicit consideration of race in admissions, policy makers have been scrambling to generate alternatives that will help the state's higher educational system serve all its residents. Thus, the University of California is complementing its state educational master plan that offers admission to the top 12.5 percent of students statewide with a plan that guarantees the top 4 percent from any school a place in the university system and another plan that would guarantee provisional admission to the top 12.5 percent of students at every high school.[5] Like a similar plan in Texas, this gives those who strive and work hard, even in poorly resourced districts, a better shot at gaining university entrance. University of California President Richard Atkinson, himself a cognitive psychologist and founding chair of the National Research Council's Board on Testing and Assessment, recently delivered a stronger signal of the welcome mat by announcing his intention to eliminate the Scholastic Assessment Test— considered by many minorities to be a biased measure of student potential—from consideration in the admissions decision.[6]

A full exploration of education would require several volumes, and we heartily acknowledge that debates over strategies and methods will continue to occupy the attention of activists, politicians, teachers, parents, and policy makers for years to come. In our view, a reasonable set of policies to tackle racial disparities in education would start with the expectation that all children can achieve at high levels and would include equalization of tax revenues by district to ameliorate inequality in spending and outcomes; enhanced teacher training to increase effectiveness with a changing population; equalization of teacher quality across schools through both training programs and financial incentives to attract experienced master instructors;[7] involvement of local communities and parents in school councils as well as other forms of community based schools that invoke community building principles; a commitment to bilingual education where appropriate for student development; full support for special English language development programs for immigrant students when needed; new spending to improve the school facilities in inner-city communities; increased outreach and affirmative action programs for college admission; and a variety of other measures.[8] While we understand the appeal of voucher

programs for racial minorities—when individual situations
are desperate, individual solutions seem necessary—the
evidence on educational outcomes is mixed; we worry
about the potential for eroding the commitment to public
education and note that voters are increasingly rejecting
voucher schemes.

Of course, many other policies are necessary to get education as a whole back on the right track, including appropriate school accountability, better teacher preparation,
etc.; our concern here has been with the relationship
between education and race. In this regard, there is a basis
for hope in the emerging agreement that the universal concern of improving all of America's schools (partly to
enhance the country's competitive profile in the world
economy) should be coupled with particular strategies and
monies for those most in need. Such "targeting within universalism" is exactly the sort of elixir we have recom-
mended.

Sprawl: A New Civil Rights Issue

The social and economic distinctions between racial and
ethnic groups have often assumed geographic shape: a
division in the fortunes of largely minority central cities and
mostly white suburbs. The pattern is not absolute: there has
been a modest suburbanization of black Americans and
Latinos,[9] and there is an increasing tendency of Asian
immigrants to locate in suburban ports of entry, such as
Monterey Park in southern California (Hum and Zonta,
2000).[10] Still, many minorities are not moving far, heading
instead to older so-called inner-ring suburbs a jurisdiction
away. For example, Compton is technically a suburb of Los
Angeles but its ethnic composition and economic despair—
roughly split between African Americans and Latinos, and
experiencing a poverty rate twice that of the rest of Los
Angeles County—suggest a clear affinity with the South
Central L.A. community that it borders.

The geographic separation has led some to believe that

they can simply leave the problems of the central city behind. However, new analyses stress that the fates of cities and suburbs in America's metropolitan regions are bound together (Peirce et al, 1993; Pastor et al., 2000). Individual escape to outlying areas, it turns out, is a temporary solution to central-city challenges: while the growth and per capita income performance of U.S. regions has diverged more and more over the past two decades (see Barnes and Ledebur, 1998), the income levels of cities and suburbs *within* the same region have converged (Savitch et al., 1993). Many of the problems of poverty have also crept into the closest inner-ring suburbs, as evidenced by the Compton example above.

Moreover, the same dynamic that has scattered jobs and housing to the detriment of city dwellers is causing stress and misery even for those in more distant suburbs. The multiworker households needed to afford a suburban piece of the American dream, the two-hour commutes required to traverse poorly planned developments, and the rising wave of youth alienation evidenced by worrisome outbreaks of school violence, all suggest that something is desperately wrong with the current pattern of regional growth.

Some analysts (Orfield, 1997; Katz, 2000) argue that this dynamic has opened the possibility for new coalitions of inner-city minorities, white workers in older suburbs, and leaders of stressed "inner-ring" municipalities, especially around regional tax-sharing mechanisms that can redirect resources from the "exurbs"—the most far-flung and economically well-off outlying areas. In fact, the coalitional possibilities of a new regionalism are even more dramatic. Environmentalists have noted how the desire to move yet another suburb away is leading to the rapid consumption of open space, with shrinking farmland and deteriorating natural conditions as the consequence. Business, once a proponent of outward expansion, has begun to worry about the patchwork of municipal government regulations, transportation inefficiencies, and fragmented training programs; in some regions, such as Charlotte, NC, and the Silicon Valley in northern California, business has led the charge for a new regional approach. Those concerned about equity, environment, and economy may be able to find new common ground.

The linkage of these issues and constituencies is increasingly occurring under the rubric of "smart growth." In Maryland, for example, "smart growth" legislation is attempting to end the practice by which developers are not required to pay the full cost of extending infrastructure to new developments; internalizing the expense of this previously provided public good has tended to shift growth back to older, core areas. In Portland, OR, urban growth boundaries have constrained developments in the periphery and led to a renaissance for key inner-city communities. In California, State Treasurer Phil Angelides has begun an active campaign to steer both public and private investment funds to the central city, partly to relieve development pressures on agriculture and environmentally sensitive land.

The potential upside for racial equity is clear: limiting sprawl and redirecting growth to the center could yield significant benefits for minority communities of all shades—including lower-income Asians who are often concentrated in central cities. Some of the needed policies are already underway in at least a pilot form, and others are politically and technically feasible. For example, a new experimental program, the location-efficient mortgage, allows borrowers near public transportation lines to claim reduced expenses and hence take out a mortgage with less money down; while racially neutral on its face, this program is especially helpful to asset building for minority homeseekers in transit-rich areas. The Intermodal Surface Transportation Equity Act (ISTEA) and its newer incarnation, TEA-21, have provided some funds to encourage reverse commutes to jobs in the suburbs, a feature that can help minority inner-city residents connect to employment; more along these lines could be done. Many areas have tried inclusionary zoning in order to spur affordable housing and desegregate the poor, and this should also be a part of state and federal housing strategies. The federal government could help by providing incentives for city and suburban cooperation in land use planning. As previously noted, infrastructure spending at all levels of government should be directed to central cities, seeking to restore their key role as anchors for regions.

Perhaps the most hopeful aspect of the "smart growth" movement is the possibility it raises for new coalitions and new politics. In Chicago, Portland, Milwaukee, and elsewhere, multiracial movements have linked the interests of suburbanites tired of traffic congestion with those of central-city residents eager for local development. In northwest Indiana—one of the most racially segregated areas in the country—a coalition of interfaith groups has brought together white Americans, African Americans, and Latinos from both central-city and suburban communities in order to oppose sprawl, argue for the deconcentration of low- and moderate-income housing, and oppose the development of suburban industries when reinvestment is desperately needed in the area's older cities. And in Columbus, OH, an inner-city group originally focused on improving public transit to its communities was able to secure the support of business groups who recognized the need for facilitating worker connections to available employment (see PolicyLink, 2000). In these kinds of activities, the principle of voice and participation mentioned in chapter 4 comes to life as communities organize to bring about change.

While such coalitions are multiracial, they must necessarily raise the uncomfortable issue of race: getting to the universal requires some attention to the particular. After all, racial avoidance has been one of the factors driving sprawl. Government policy has subsidized the choice, providing federal and state spending on highways to the suburbs, mortgage interest deductions that encouraged larger homes, and local zoning laws that limited density, while failing central-city school quality also pushed along the exo-

dus. Still, race is part of the picture at both the level of individual choice and governmental policy.

But even as race must be lifted, the "smart growth"
bandwagon has a universalist advantage: it appeals to common interest and it gives participants of all colors a concrete set of tasks and issues to work on, such as agreements
about sewer lines, zoning laws, or transit investments,
rather than vague discussions of the need for brotherhood.
The scale of the region is also an advantage. At the federal
level, it may be easy to deny public funding for a midnight
basketball league; as participants in a regional conversation
come together face to face and race to race, it is harder to
ignore one another's agendas and communities.

While the usual assumption is that the reluctant partners in such a conversation would be satisfied suburbanites, minority communities and their leaders are often
worried that their interests will be lost and their numbers
overwhelmed should they join in a larger regional
approach. Moreover, resteering growth to the central city
has often produced gentrification, with longer-term
minority residents forced out by higher housing costs. But
if the future of America is regional, then minority leaders
must understand the changing politics of scale and work to
ensure that "smart growth" becomes not just urban
boundaries and the protection of open space but also the
active promotion of local ownership, job connections, and
the housing needed by lower-income residents. Such
"equitable development"[11] strategies will be key to realizing the multiracial and pangeographic alliances promised
by the new antisprawl movement.

Environmental Justice

The process of sprawl and inner-city decline has tended to
contribute to another key new issue: environmental justice.[12] As industries have moved away from many minority
central-city communities, firms have frequently left behind
contaminated sites that remain economically fallow because

of liability concerns. Other toxic land uses, such as storage and disposal facilities for the wastes produced by manufacturing processes or the refining of petroleum products, are located in areas that are disproportionately poor and minority. Native Americans face their own version of environmental inequities with problems related to strip mining and medical waste incinerators experienced by various reservations (Robyn and Camacho, 1998).

Against this backdrop has emerged a movement of local groups determined to protect their health and neighborhood integrity. In 1991, many of these groups came together for the first National People of Color Environmental Leadership Summit and adopted principles of environmental justice. In 1994, two years after an EPA study concluded that there was indeed a potential problem of racial disparity in environmental exposure, President Clinton issued an executive order directing all agencies to adopt environmental justice as a principal policy concern.[13]

Not everyone has bought into the notion of a correlation of color and toxicity. A series of studies launched by researchers at the University of Massachusetts found that there was little evidence that race was related to hazardous facilities once researchers controlled for income, proximity to manufacturing employees, and other explanatory variables (see, for example, Anderton et al., 1994). However, one of the newest and most careful national studies—conducted by researchers initially skeptical about the claims of minority community organizations—has concluded that race is indeed a significant independent predictor of the incidence of environmental negatives (Lester et al., 2001).

This conclusion squares with the mounting evidence from other studies. For example, Morello-Frosch et al. (2001) looked at whether there were racial disparities in lifetime cancer risk from hazardous air pollution in southern California, an area that is among the most polluted in the country. Accounting for location, wind, toxicity, and

FIGURE 5-7. Distribution of Estimated Lifetime Cancer Risk From Ambient Hazardous Air Pollutant Exposures by Race/Ethnicity and Income, Southern California

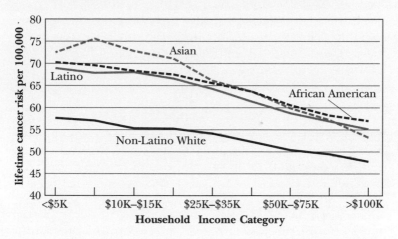

other measures, they found a striking pattern: while the overexposure of minorities was highest in the lower-income levels, there was a divergent pattern by race that continued even into households with very high income levels (see Figure 5-7).

Environmental justice is an issue that marries the universal and the particular. Everyone gains from cleaner air and water, but given the current pattern, the positive impacts of stricter pollution standards would lend especially needed relief to minority communities. Moreover, alleviating the special environmental burden on minorities may relax the burden on all. Morello-Frosch's 1997 study of environmental inequalities throughout California suggests that those counties that have the most inequality in incomes and exposure actually also have higher levels of hazardous air. The implication: when it is easier to place hazards in someone else's backyard, the overall level of hazards will rise. One route to achieving a healthier environment for everyone is to target those areas that are currently exposed at a disproportionate level.

How is environmental justice operationalized? One key element is enhanced public outreach and access as agencies make decisions about placing what are termed LULUs—locally undesirable land uses. But outreach is not enough—it is hard to expect communities that do not have enough political power to then be sufficiently organized to respond to threats. Because of this, regulators should consider both demographic conditions and current exposure levels and develop rules that can "greenline" certain areas so that they will be off-limits for future siting (see Pastor et al., 2001).

Currently exposed communities should also be adequately compensated, including first crack at the opportunity to transform contaminated lands or "brownfields" into productive economic assets. Of special interest will be programs to protect the health of minority children, particularly as new public schools to accommodate burgeoning immigrant populations are sited in dense urban areas often experiencing intense levels of air pollution as well as proximity to hazardous wastes. While a full set of policies will necessarily await further research and discussion, this issue will likely continue its rise onto the civil rights agenda. The country must make the goal of a safe environment a reality for all Americans.

The Digital Divide: More Than Just Computers

While recent years have brought some progress, there is still a persistent racial differential in computer ownership and Internet use (see Figures 5-8 and 5-9).

Often termed the "digital divide," this gap has focused much attention on strategies that promote access. The digital divide, however, is about more than access. While education and income are typically cited as the key factors

FIGURE 5-8. Percent of U.S. Households with Computers, 1994–2000

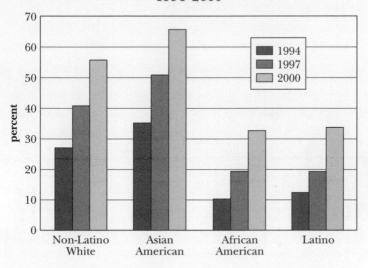

FIGURE 5-9. Percent of U.S. Households with Access to the Internet, 1997–2000

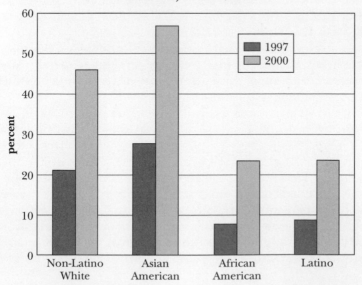

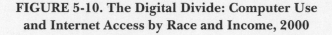

**FIGURE 5-10. The Digital Divide: Computer Use
and Internet Access by Race and Income, 2000**

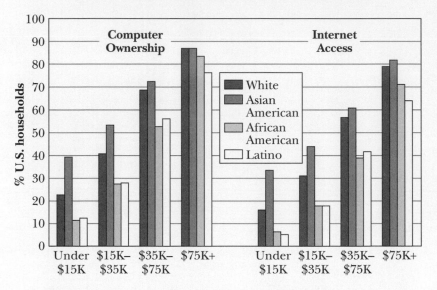

affecting access, the fact remains that racial differences in computer and Internet use exist at all income brackets (see Figure 5-10).

As a result, analysts have begun to focus on the relevance of content, including whether sites offer appropriate cultural materials or provide useful information on economic opportunities or education.[14]

Access is clearly an issue for Native Americans, particularly those living in far-flung reservations that often lack telephone service, let alone high-speed hook-ups to the Internet.[15] Bridging this gap could hold special promise for America's First Peoples: the Internet can connect geographically dispersed communities and provide economies of scale for producing and distributing Native American programming. There are examples of successful projects throughout the country, ranging from the Hawaii Community College two-way video conferencing among several islands, to the use of distance learning in Alaska above the Arctic Circle, to the fiber optic wiring to government offices and community centers of the Oneida Nation in New York state.[16]

The disparities that exist, however, go beyond access. The digital economy is reinforcing historical, social, and economic inequalities at several levels. For example, one of the issues that must be addressed is the racial disparity that exists in employment in an industry that has some of the best-paying jobs. In Silicon Valley, the heart of the digital revolution, the demographics of the resident population have been majority-minority for several years—but the ranks of software engineers, corporate executives, and systems managers remain predominantly white (and sometimes Asian).[17] At a higher level, color blanches further: a 1998 survey of forty-nine leading companies in the Silicon Valley found that there were just two African Americans and one Latino in a group of 364 board members.[18]

Some leaders in the Silicon Valley argue that disparities in the outcomes in the high-tech industry reflect talent, not discrimination. Yet a recent study of over 700 MBAs (Dreher and Cox, 2000) directly challenges the notion of a "meritocracy," even at the top end of the labor market. While all the MBAs examined were from top-flight programs and roughly of the same age group, the authors found that white males who jumped from their firms to another tended to raise their salary twice as much as minorities who moved (even after controlling for the usual factors such as time spent in the current job, any periods of unemployment, and placement in different sectors of the economy). While some of this may be outright discrimination, another key factor is very different social networks. These networks, in turn, lead to differential information flows about the best jobs and differential opportunities for better employment—and current inequities become reproduced even without individual intention.

Another factor may be the shortage of qualified minority applicants. According to the U.S. Department of Labor, only 9 percent of U.S. degrees in engineering and com-

puter science are earned by African Americans or Latinos—
despite the rapidly growing need for such high-tech workers.[19] Companies that groan about problems of labor
shortage are beginning to see the connection: while labor
shortfalls can be temporarily solved with an appeal for H1-
B visas for qualified foreign workers, the longer-run solution involves the nurturing of "home-grown" talent,
particularly of minority youngsters who often steer away
from computer careers. Addressing racial disparity in technology jobs makes business as well as social sense.[20]

What should be done? Some efforts are focusing on connecting low-income people to technology jobs building on
the fact that 40 percent of these jobs do not require a college degree. A recent report by Chapple (2000), *From
Promising Practices to Promising Futures*, reviews some of these
programs. Keys to success are strong relationships to industry both for designing relevant curriculum and insuring job
placement, a regional approach since this is the scale of the
industry itself, and the integration of "soft skills" and technical training appropriate to the IT industry. One industry-
spawned initiative that is actively training individuals to
participate in the booming networking industry is the Cisco
Academy program: the demand for graduates is strong, the
pay is high, and the educational requirements suit those
who choose not to go to college (see Box 5-1).

A more community oriented effort is the Bay Area Video
Coalition in San Francisco and its JobLink program to train
and place low-income individuals. Both the community
based and industry initiated training programs should be
scaled up—a task that will require both corporate and
foundation support.

Another way to address disparities is via technology centers at a community level. Such centers, like Plugged-In in
East Palo Alto, provide a place where young and old alike
can be trained to use computers to meet everyday needs
(see Box 5-2).

The East Austin (TX) Community Network supports fifteen outpost sites for residents to gain access to and learn to

Box 5-1. Cisco Kids

The Cisco Networking Academy's new model for learning was introduced in October 1997. The program, global in its scope, offers a 560-hour (eight-semester) hands-on curriculum that teaches Internet and technology literacy along with specific skills such as network principles, building, and maintenance. The e-learning model delivers Web-based educational content, online testing, student performance tracking, hands-on labs, and instructor training and support. According to Cisco the growth of the academies has far exceeded its initial expectations: as of summer 2000, more than 153,700 students were enrolled, and there were an estimated 10,000 graduates.

The academies are taught mainly in high schools (public and private) and community colleges where students complete the courses knowing how to design, build, and manage computer networks. Technology support is offered for schools that lack the current resources, with the academies made possible by an investment of $20 million by Cisco Systems and the Cisco Foundation as well as valuable sponsors and partnerships with various suppliers, training developers, curriculum developers, or membership organizations. For example, there is a Cisco-Microsoft educational partnership that offers a complete range of complementary training services from the lower-level networking services provided by integrated hardware and software products known as switches and routers to the higher-level networking services that allow users to share information and resources and have e-mail access.

The strength of the program is that it is teaching a highly marketable set of skills around network infrastructure to disadvantaged and at-risk students throughout the world. The company even presents occasional workshops for children, including one to the San Jose–based

Unity Care Group Inc., which prepares youth to pursue professions in which minorities are underrepresented. Another example of outreach into underserved communities is through the Camp Sweeny program for youth. Camp Sweeny is a detention center in Hayward, CA, in which students who pass the GED exam are allowed to enroll in the Cisco Networking Academy. The interest has been so great that some students, even after being discharged from the center, have returned to complete the program and exam. Some students who had little direction in terms of their future careers found the academy opened up great opportunities for them, allowing them to clarify their goals and stay out of the detention center. There is a similar project in a correctional facility in Gainesville, TX, that gives youth tools to reenter society after incarceration.

This is a remarkable program—one that has met the needs of both business and the community. On the business side, the supply of technically savvy network technicians is expanding, addressing the dramatic shortage of information technology workers. But because these are well-paying jobs that require relatively modest training, the Cisco Networking Academy Program is also helping previously underserved populations build digital bridges to the Internet economy.

use the Internet, with sites ranging from the library to an apartment complex to churches and policy centers. The best programs bridge the gap by illustrating how the computer can be a tool for economic life—from balancing your checkbook to starting a business.[21]

While it is necessary to continue to focus on connecting low-income people to jobs in the digital economy, it should also be recognized that computer related jobs are only a handful of the twenty occupations likely to generate the

Box 5-2. Plugging In to the New Economy

In the 1960s, Timothy Leary called for America to "tune in, turn on, and drop out." The call for the new millennium might be "plug in, log on, and reach out." Access to information technology and the relevant tools/skills to go with it are the cornerstones for realizing individual potential, but they can also be key to the building of community. Recognizing both the need and the opportunity, a new community technology movement is seeking to tackle the digital divide and use the Internet and its tools for the amelioration of poverty and racism.

One such organization has successfully tackled the digital divide in the poorest city located in what may be the region with the largest inequality gap in the nation. Lodged in the heart of Silicon Valley, East Palo Alto is a low-income community that, according to the 1990 census, was 41 percent African American, 36 percent Latino, 12 percent Caucasian, 9 percent Asian/Pacific Islanders, and 2 percent "other." Stressed by high housing costs, significant high school dropout rates, and unemployment levels that are three times higher than the rest of the county, East Palo Alto's low-income and even middle-income residents are struggling to keep up with the economic forces of the technology boom despite their proximity to the heart of the Silicon revolution.

Since 1992 Plugged In, a community technology center with a mission to ensure that everyone in East Palo Alto has the opportunity to fully benefit from the information revolution, has reached out to the city's disadvantaged youth and families. The organization offers three main programs to help improve the economic, social, professional, and educational opportunities for community members, especially youth: Plugged In Enterprises, which trains teenagers in Web design, allowing them to build the necessary skills to work for community members and commercial clients such as Pacific Bell and Sun

Microsystems; Plugged In Greenhouse, a creative arts
and technology studio that has a variety of activities
including an afterschool program, classroom partnerships, and special projects based on educational themes;
and the Technology Access Center, which provides access
to computers and the Internet through its community
production studio, copy center, cyber library, self-paced
learning studio, and telecom center.

Their work goes beyond training. For example, Plugged
In staff help people with job searches and provide health
related information, homework assistance, and refer-
ences for starting a small business. These programs
make up a comprehensive menu of educational services
enabling residents to improve their skills for securing
quality employment in the technology sector. By combining skill building and relevance, Plugged In is doing its
part to bridge the digital divide in the U.S. society and
economy. For more information, naturally there's a web
site: www.pluggedin.org.

most new jobs in the U.S. economy over the coming decade
(see Table 5-1).[22]

Nationally, there will actually be more new jobs that pay
"very low" wages, as indicated by their earnings in 1998,
than new jobs that pay "very high" wages. Many of these
low-wage jobs, including retail sales, janitors, waiters/wait-
resses, and guards, are actually part of servicing the new
economy of professionals: every software engineer requires
a crew of nannies, food servers, and housekeepers living at
the low end in order to make their own mark at the high
end. The process is particularly accelerated in California,
where three of the six occupations with the greatest projected growth—accounting for nearly half of the new jobs

TABLE 5-1
**Projected Occupational Growth in the U.S. Economy,
Top Twenty Occupations, 1998–2008**

Occupation title	Employment change, 1998–2008	1998 Median earnings quartile rank
Systems analysts	577,319	Very High
Retail salespersons	563,204	Very Low
All other sales and related workers	557,718	High
Cashiers	556,210	Very Low
General managers and top executives	550,801	Very High
Truck drivers light and heavy	492,997	High
Office clerks, general	463,115	Low
Registered nurses	450,864	Very High
Computer support specialists	439,358	Very High
Personal care and home health aides	433,414	Very Low
Teacher assistants	375,098	Very Low
Janitors and cleaners, including maids and housekeeping cleaners	365,212	Very Low
Nursing aides, orderlies, and attendants	324,915	Very Low
Computer engineers	322,805	Very High
Teachers, secondary school	322,316	Very High
Office and administrative support supervisors and managers	312,758	High
All other managers and administrators	305,465	Very High
Receptionists and information clerks	305,423	Low
Waiters and waitresses	303,254	Very Low
Guards	294,074	Very Low

Source: Bureau of Labor Statistics, *Occupational Outlook Handbook, 2000–2001;* see
ftp://146.142.4.23/pub/special.requests/ep/OPTDdata/optd9808.txt

in that group—offer pay that places them into the lowest quartile of jobs by earnings.[23]

In short, the issue is not really the digital divide; it is the divide in the digital economy. While training low-skilled workers to move up the job ladder is important and remains central to any program of economic and racial justice, it is necessary to ensure that basic service jobs have the wage, health insurance, and retirement packages needed for workers to provide for themselves and their families. Since so many of the employees in these positions are minority, the strategies to do this—increasing the minimum wage, expanding the Earned Income Tax Credit, elaborating a health insurance safety net, facilitating worker representation via unionization—are all civil rights frontiers for the future. Our orienting principle—one which is universal but will have particular benefits—is that lifting the bottom of the labor market should be done through both appropriate training for emerging tech jobs in the economy and higher standards for the continuing profusion of basic service employment.

Immigrant Policy

The title of this section was chosen with intent: too much time has been spent on immigration policy and too little time on immigrant policy.

As noted above, the U.S. economy is generating a demand for both high-skilled and low-skilled labor—and it is a demand that domestic workers do not fully meet. At one end of the spectrum, an influx of Asian engineers and entrepreneurs is helping the Silicon Valley retain its role as the center of the world's Internet and electronic industries (Saxenian, 1999). At another end, Mexican and other Latino immigrants are not only fueling the traditional economic engine of agriculture but also have become the dominant group working in manufacturing in places like Los Angeles and have seen their presence skyrocket in meat packing and textile areas of the South.

The usual policy focus is on whether and how to control

FIGURE 5-11. Percent of U.S. Population Foreign-Born, 1950–1999

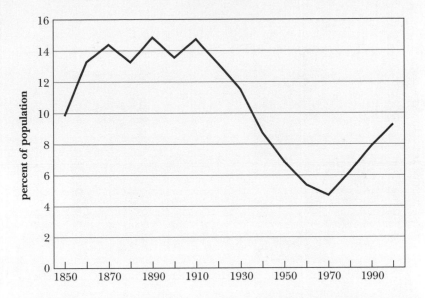

the flow of immigrants. As can be seen in Figure 5-11, the percentage foreign born is still below the peak achieved in the late 19th and early 20th centuries, but the increases over the past thirty years have been dramatic.

The sharp fall prior to this, during the first half of the century, was due to tightening of immigration restrictions via the quota system of 1918 and the 1924 Immigration Act, both of which also worked to limit immigration from areas other than Great Britain and northern Europe, partly because of racial animus toward those from other parts of Europe and the rest of the world. The steady decrease in the percentage of foreign born was turned around only after a new immigration law in 1965 relaxed restrictions, particularly on immigrants from Latin America and Asia.

The impacts of this relaxation can be seen in the change in the composition of the foreign born between 1970 and

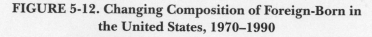

FIGURE 5-12. Changing Composition of Foreign-Born in the United States, 1970–1990

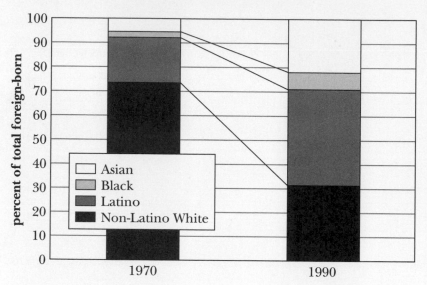

1990 depicted in Figure 5-12: the Latino, black, and Asian shares of this population have grown at extraordinary rates over that twenty-year period, and the final figures for the 2000 census are likely to show an even further shift in the foreign-born mix.

Some, including Peter Brimelow (1995) in his influential book *Alien Nation*, have expressed concern that the current trend will dilute what he sees as the essentially Anglo-Saxon character of U.S culture and society. Others, like George Borjas (1999) of Harvard, focus on "immigrant quality" and argue that the influx of lower-skill immigrants will swamp the bottom end of the labor market, making it more difficult for African Americans and U.S.-born Latinos to make their way out of poverty.

The economic evidence is still the subject of debate, and the discussion of "quality" has raised egalitarian hackles—particularly in light of the 1990 immigration reform that allows individuals promising to invest $1 million in the

United States to secure a visa, a policy shift that has led to charges that migration status is being auctioned to the highest bidder. In any case, it seems that those hurt least by immigrant competition are high-skilled whites for whom low-skill workers are complements, not substitutes; those helped least are U.S.-born Latinos and African Americans who often compete in the same labor markets as new arrivals. Strikingly, public opinion polls often run the exact opposite of the economic effects: Latinos and Asians are generally the most pro-immigrant, with white Americans most resistant, and African Americans in the middle.

Our concern is on immigrants, not immigration. While there is an ongoing debate about "manageable" levels of migration and significant public attention on the level of undocumented immigration, there is little possibility, beyond full-scale militarization of the border, to seriously staunch the flow from Mexico. Moreover, the gains are clear: immigrants have helped revitalize inner-city and other communities, are fueling key portions of the high-tech industry, and are creating a new civic life (Grogan and Proscio, 2000). In short, immigrants are here to stay. The question is how best to facilitate their economic and social assimilation into the United States, particularly given their relatively large numbers.

One key on that front is ensuring that the children of immigrants, who are often U.S. born, receive adequate public education and services—even when their parents have uncertain legal status.[24] Here, the lessons from unexpected places experiencing new immigration might be instructive: the Georgia Project mentioned in Box 5-3 inspired Senator Max Cleland to sponsor the still-pending Immigrants to New Americans Act that would steer federal Department of Education grants to communities affected by new immigration; it would also help provide immigrant families with access to other comprehensive services such as healthcare, childcare, job training, and transportation.

Ideas to improve the experience of immigrant school children include expanding the class day to afford students the time to learn both English and academic subjects and improving academic assessment tools for English learners

Box 5-3. Grace of Unexpected Places

Immigrant location is not what economists call a "random walk"—Los Angeles and New York alone receive nearly 22 percent of all the legal immigrants to the nation (a figure that would likely rise if we were to include undocumented migration). Partly as a result, Latinos are strikingly concentrated: 70 percent of the entire U.S. Latino population now lives in California, Texas, Florida, New York, and Illinois.

Figure for Box 5-3. U.S. Latinos by Geographic Location

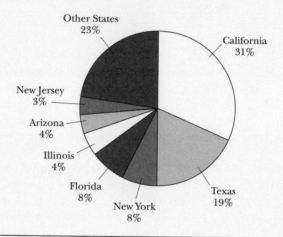

As we noted in chapter 2, the Latino population is now growing rapidly in areas once unaccustomed to a Latino presence. For example, of the twenty U.S. counties with the fastest growing Latino populations, seven were in Arkansas and seven in Georgia, with the remainder mostly in the more traditional locations—Florida, Texas, and Illinois. The reason for the growing population is largely work related: in industries such as poultry and carpet-making, Latino immigrants have become the workers of employer choice.

In Dalton, GA, a town of about 22,000, one school is already 80 percent Latino, and the district is 45 percent Latino. The school board, partly under pressure from business, has started the Georgia Project, a program that sends twenty Dalton educators to Mexico every summer. While there has been some anger about the transformation of rural Georgia, positive signs of community support are reflected in programs such as the Georgia Project, and Latinos report that the reception from the local African American community has been especially warm.

Whether these attitudes will withstand an economic downturn is yet to be seen, but in the meantime, the willingness to actively welcome assimilation and consider new creative policy to help this along is striking. With attention shifted from restricting immigration to incorporating immigrants, tensions have been reduced and local economies have benefited. We all may have much to learn from the grace of unexpected places.

so that they are able to be appropriately placed by ability (see Fix and Zimmerman, 2000).

While elementary and secondary school programs can be designed to better meet the needs of immigrant children, it is important to note community colleges could, in this millennium, play the role that "settlement houses" played for European immigrants at the turn of the 19th century. While the broader adult education system attempts to provide English as a second language (ESL) and other practical skills, and ESL students have risen from 17 percent of adult education students in 1980 to 48 percent in 1998 (Fix and Zimmerman, 2000), the community college system holds the affordable keys to real job training and advancement.

Other institutions and organizations can play a role. Labor is a particularly important actor, given the working-class character of many immigrants of color. The news in this regard is heartening: the AFL-CIO has, for example, abandoned a long-held position in favor of sanctions against employers hiring undocumented immigrants, in part because this policy has impeded the trust needed to organize immigrant workers regardless of documentation status. In general, workers should feel safe to unionize and otherwise improve their condition regardless of migration status—and the government can help by securing whistleblower laws that prevent firms from calling immigration authorities in order to disrupt worker self-organization.

Other community based institutions are important to immigrant assimilation. Legal centers can provide advice on immigration, but also on tenant rights and other skills needed to navigate in the U.S. political system. Community health centers can provide preventive education and ensure quick access to those who may lack insurance. Local planning agencies could commit to involve all residents in neighborhood design efforts; there are no restrictions imposed in such processes regarding citizenship, and such exercises could be active training ground for an engaged future citizen.

The federal government should play a role in setting equitable and fair policies for immigrants. It may be useful to break the Immigration and Naturalization Service (INS) itself into two agencies: one focused on border and immigration law enforcement, the other on programs for immigrants once they are here. This could change the face of the INS and encourage more residents to depend on its help and expertise as they and their children make a smooth transition in contemporary society. Such a shift could be accompanied by a new amnesty for undocumented immigrants, allowing for a fresh start even as the country's dependence on immigrant labor is recognized. The central point: it is important to develop new strategies for full incorporation of immigrants into a changing America.

Crime and Punishment

The United States has the highest rate of imprisonment in the world—surpassing Russia, the only other country that comes close to rivaling the U.S. level. There is a definite hue to those imprisoned: as Figure 5-13 shows, nearly 7 percent of all black males in the United States were in federal or state prisons or local jails in 1997 (a near doubling in the rate from 3.5 percent in 1985).

The nation's capital leads the states with the highest rate: a black man is forty-nine times more likely than a white man to be in prison.[25]

U.S. minorities are also far more likely to be the victims of crime, and countless other personal and property crimes make daily life a challenge in inner-city neighborhoods throughout the country. But the high rates of incarceration are not due solely to proximity to, or participation in, crime. There is a racial bias in the criminal justice system as borne

FIGURE 5-13. Percent of Adult Males Held in Federal or State Prisons and Local Jails, 1985–1997

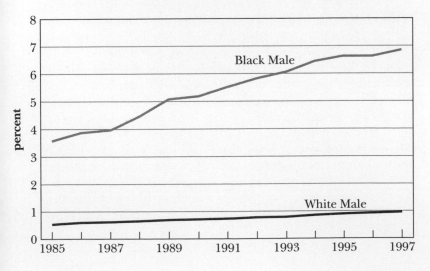

out by the following: analyzing national and state data, researchers have recently determined that while African Americans represent 15 percent of those below the age of eighteen, they are 26 percent of all the young arrested, 46 percent of those detained in juvenile jails, and 58 percent of all juveniles sent to adult prison (Poe-Yamagata and Jones, 2000). Young white men charged with violent offenses have an average imprisonment of 193 days after trial; for African American and Latino youth, the figures are 254 and 305 days, respectively (Marable, 2000). Similarly, black adults receive longer sentences than whites for convictions for the same crime, even when whites have more past offenses.

A recent study by Building Blocks for Youth may explain a part of this bias. The study (Dorfman and Schiraldi, 2001) found that at a time of falling crime rates among youth of color, the news media overemphasize crimes committed by these young people, distorting reality and leading to a false perception of their role in criminal acts.

The war on drugs has also played a role in the darkening of the prison population. From 1980 to 1998, the percentage of state prisoners incarcerated for drug related offenses increased from 6 percent to 21 percent; during this same period, the percentage of prisoners incarcerated for violent crimes decreased from 59 percent to 48 percent, suggesting that drug offenders were "crowding out" truly dangerous felons. Of the nation's drug offenders, 62.7 percent are black, though there are five times more white drug users than black. Part of the reason is the stiffer penalties for crack cocaine (more commonly associated with black drug users) than for powder cocaine (more commonly associated with white drug users), despite the fact that the drugs are pharmacologically identical. The structure of criminal enforcement tends to reinforce the arrest pattern by targeting the low-income neighborhoods where the drug trade may flourish rather than the suburban areas (or university campuses) where many consumers reside.

In high-crime neighborhoods that are racially segregated and socially isolated, imprisonment or the constant threat of imprisonment strains community social networks. Jail time becomes a rite of passage—an expected part of growing up.[26] Since rehabilitation has been de-emphasized in the spirit of "getting tough" on both crime and individuals, prisoners are often unprepared to re-enter the outside world and return to criminal activities and jail. Even for those who are not even convicted, there are debilitating financial drains from relentless legal fees, raising bail, and the income forgone from lost jobs and a fragmented work history.

With prisons and jails occupying a central role in the lives of inner-city residents and evidence mounting of differential patterns of arrest and jailing, distrust of the police becomes standard: according to a 1999 survey, 42 percent of black Americans believed they were stopped just because of their race or ethnicity (see Figure 5-14), and 77 percent of blacks believe that racial profiling, the tendency of police officers to assume that people of color commit certain types of crimes, is widespread.[27]

The result has been a tense relationship with police in

FIGURE 5-14. Experience of Racial Profiling, 1999

Have you ever felt that you were stopped by the police just because of your race?

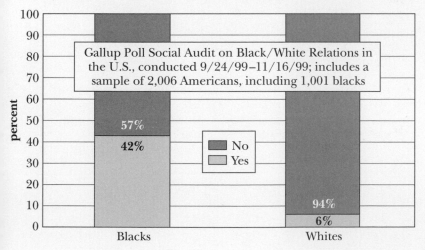

many communities. This tension is made worse when shootings of unarmed black residents, as in Cincinnati in April 2001, trigger social tension and upheaval.

Changing course on both the criminal justice front and the police-community front will require a rethinking of current strategies as well as political courage. For example, the country needs to reconsider the harsh sentences handed to so many who would benefit from drug treatment rather than jail time and specifically address the disparity in sentencing between crack and powder cocaine. The juvenile justice system, which has become a feeder system for prisons, should become less punitive and focus more on rehabilitation and re-entry. So should the adult system: while it was politically popular to cut off inmate eligibility for federal Pell Grant loans (Marable, 2000), studies have found that prisoners who are able to complete a college degree while serving time are much less likely to be recidivist. Voting rights for ex-felons should be restored as a way to help re-integrate these individuals into society and aid in their contribution to the civic life of communities. The public will for such a reform can be marshaled, as witnessed by the recent repeal of a felon disenfranchisement law in Connecticut, allowing convicted felons on probation to vote (Zielbauer, 2001).

New strategies are needed that focus on reducing the plague of crime in urban communities—but in ways that do not further strain community-police relations. A fuller commitment to community-centered policing could help. Policies here include increasing the diversity of local police forces, establishing independent boards to review police misconduct, and gathering information about police stops that can help policy makers determine and then correct trends of racial profiling (see PolicyLink, 2001b). Such strategies will not necessarily grate on the sensibilities of police officers, many of whom recognize that fortifying their relations with community leaders and residents will make their jobs easier, not harder.

This may be one of the toughest areas for change—and one of the biggest challenges for leadership. The federal government should set the tone for equitable and fair policies in this arena. America must face up to the fact that too many people of color are imprisoned—and accept that this is a crisis that requires immediate attention. Leaders must be willing to question the current ethos of punishment and tackle reform of hallowed institutions like the police. Most important, leaders must be willing to point out that while attention to racial disparities in criminal justice outcomes may seem like a particularistic strategy, new policies may help lower costs in prison construction and maintenance, brake some of the forces fragmenting families, and enable more people to contribute to continued economic prosperity.

Conclusion

The issues we have highlighted—education, sprawl, environmental justice, the divide in the digital economy, immigrant incorporation, and criminal justice—are not exhaustive. Voting rights is an issue of renewed importance, and the redrawing of electoral districts in light of the 2000 census figures will be a battleground for minority interests. Health disparities are likely to be another important issue, particularly given the dramatic differences in health insurance evidenced in chapter 3. While our list may be incomplete, the issues covered here are important and signal a few key aspects of a future civil rights agenda for America.

Perhaps most significantly, the issues facing America in the 21st century may be different, deeper, and more complex than the questions of overt discrimination that occupied attention in an earlier era. Approaching them successfully will require looking for universal gains and principles—such as everyone's right to a clean environment or the common interest in restraining sprawl—even as the particularities of effects on different ethnic groups are understood and addressed. Policy recommendations will require serious research and honest debate rather than a simple attachment to old remedies.

We have tried to be pragmatic in this discussion, suggesting particular ways in which education might be improved, sprawl curtailed, environmental burdens shared, technology benefits spread, immigrants incorporated, and both crime and criminalization reduced. But policy alone will not be enough: what is required is a new leadership that combines moral vision and pragmatic solutions, deeply held values, a willingness to change one's mind, and an understanding of both universal appeal and particular needs.

When one thinks of leaders, one often imagines a single person who appears just in time to speak the truth and save the day. But to be sustainable, wisdom should be rooted not in any one individual but rather in a broad spectrum of community and civic leaders, all committed to improving equity as well as communication. There are and have been such leaders at all levels in U.S. society, but just as the pressing problems of racial inequality cannot be solved without purposeful action, so too will the scale of leadership needed fail to materialize unless the character traits are defined and programs are developed to nurture and support leaders as they work toward solutions. It is to this discussion that we now turn.

Notes

[1] The numbers may overstate the case a bit for Latinos, in part because the figures refer to stocks and not to flows of graduates. As a result, the Latino numbers include immigrant adults who did not complete high school and have since moved to the United States; limiting our attention to graduation rates for Latinos in the United States would improve the picture, but even the so-called event dropout rates are extraordinarily high for Latinos. Moreover, the "stock" or educational level numbers are relevant for determining likely contemporary economic and social outcomes.

[2] The data for math scores follow a similar pattern, although the gap is less severe between whites and their black and Latino counterparts, and Asians actually outpoint whites, especially in the older age groups.

[3] See Steele and Aronson (1995) and the popular review of this research in Sharon Begley, "The Stereotype Trap," *Newsweek*, November 6, 2000, pp. 66–68.

[4] A related set of Gallup polls indicates that, as of 1999, 68 percent of Americans believe that school integration has improved the quality of education received by black students and 50 percent also believe that integration improved the quality of education for white students.

[5] See Martha Groves, "UC Renews Hope for Students Who Missed Program," *Los Angeles Times*, Saturday, December 23, 2000, p. B-1, and Arenson (2000).

[6] See Kenneth R. Weiss, "UC Chief Seeks to Drop SAT as a Requirement," *Los Angeles Times*, Saturday, February 17, 2001, p. A-1.

[7] There is a significant body of emerging evidence suggesting that teacher quality matters greatly to student performance and that there are sharp inequities in the distribution of skilled teachers by both the income and racial character of student bodies, in part because of the practice of concentrating new teachers in schools with significant numbers of poor and minority children (see Haycock, 1998). For a full discussion of this topic and other issues, see The Education Trust at www.edtrust.org.

[8] We also support student leadership programs that bring together youth of different ethnicities; with the resegregation of America's schools, such cross-site efforts are increasingly necessary to build the bridges that will serve leaders well in the future.

[9] An analysis of census 2000 data reveals that the phenomenon of "flight to the suburbs" is spreading among people of color. "Minorities are moving to the nation's mostly white suburbs like never before and forming their own racial and ethnic enclaves" (Nasser, 2001). John Logan, a sociologist at the University of Albany (GA) and author of the analysis, continues, however, that "'suburbanization' of minorities doesn't necessarily mean more integration." His study of suburbs in 330 metropolitan areas revealed that more affluent minorities are choosing to live among themselves. "Upper-income blacks want to associate more with their own people because they feel more comfortable," explains political science professor William Boone of Clark Atlanta University. He maintains that as blacks gain financial and political clout, the need to integrate decreases: "We have to rethink this whole question of who wants integration and why we want integration." Demographer William Frey predicts that in melting-pot metro areas such as Los Angeles, New York, and Miami—areas that have large numbers of people of all races and ethnic backgrounds—concentration in the suburbs is temporary. "If we fast-forward to the next ten years, we'll find more intermarriages, more integration, and more assimilation," predicts Frey of the Milken Institute in Santa Monica, CA. For more details on this coloring of the suburbs and its implications, see Nasser (2001).

[10] Monterey Park is the only city outside of Hawaii with majority Asian American population, and its surrounding cities in the San Gabriel Valley of Los Angeles County have been described as a new "ethnoburb" (Li, 1999). For an excellent analysis of the changes in this community, see Saito (1998).

[11] Equitable development is a term used by PolicyLink to describe policies and practices that enable low-income and low-wealth residents to participate in and benefit from regional economic activity.

[12] See, for example, the discussion in Bullard et al. (2000) and Pastor (2001).

[13] For an excellent overview of the environmental justice movement and its principles, see Bullard (1993, 1994).

[14] On the accounting for the gap, see NTIA (1999). On the issue of more appropriate cultural content, see Tseng (2001). Both African Americans and Latinos have a high rate of visitation of ethnic websites, with African Americans expressing an even stronger preference for ethnic sites and a much lower percent of satisfaction with online content. Also, both groups have a higher tendency (43 percent for blacks and 47 percent for Latinos) than the general market (31 percent) to use the Internet for school research; obviously, the Web can be an important part of family support for education in these communities.

[15] In 2000, for example, about half of the Native American homes in rural areas did not have telephone service, significantly below national averages. See www.wws.princeton.edu:80/~ota/disk1/1995/9542._n.html.

[16] www.wws.princeton.edu:80/~ota/disk1/1995/9542_n.html.

[17] There are also potential problems in specific firms: a recent lawsuit filed by black employees of Microsoft, for example, alleges that African Americans have been systematically bypassed for relevant promotions. See Kristi Heim, "Tech Companies Invest Millions to Bring Diversity," *San Jose Mercury News*, January 15, 2001, pp. 1A, 10A.

[18] See Joel Dreyfuss, "Valley of Denial," *Fortune*, July 17, 1999.

[19] See Joel Dreyfuss, "Valley of Denial," *Fortune*, July 17, 1999.

[20] Based on this realization, some companies have made progress. Intel Corporation reports, for example, that there was a 26 percent increase in the number of employees from underrepresented groups (African Americans, Latinos, and Native Americans). See Pat Lopes Harris, "High-tech Progress on Diversity Proves Difficult to Measure Well," *San Jose Mercury News*, January 15, 2001, p. 10A.

[21] See PolicyLink (2001a) and Nelson and Servon (2001) for full discussions of the role of community technology centers and the importance of content.

[22] Even on the edge of the cyber-revolution, Silicon Valley, high technology defined in the broadest possible way accounts for only 30 percent of the jobs, with the remainder being local service and often lower wage.

[23] Estimates from the California Employment Development Department; see www.calmis.cahwnet.gov.

[24] In New York, for example, 70 percent of families with children headed by undocumented immigrants have children who are citizens. See Fix and Zimmerman (2000).

[25] See www.hrw.org/reports/2000/usa/Rcedrg00-01.htm#P149_24292.

[26] See the excellent popular article by Ellis Cose, "The Prison Paradox," *Newsweek*, November 13, 2000.

27 See the *Sourcebook of Criminal Justice Statistics*, 1999, p. 111 (available at www.albany.edu/sourcebook/1995/pdf/section2.pdf).

References

Anderton, Douglas L., Andy B. Anderson, Michael Oakes, and Michael R. Fraser. 1994. "Environmental Equity: The Demographics of Dumping." *Demography*, 31(2).

Arenson, Karen W. 2000. "California Proposal Aims to Improve College Diversity." *New York Times*, September 22.

Barnes, William, and Larry C. Ledebur. 1998. *The New Regional Economies: The U.S. Common Market and the Global Economy*. Thousand Oaks, CA: Sage Publications.

Borjas, George. 1999. *Heaven's Door: Immigration Policy and the American Economy*. Princeton, NJ: Princeton University Press.

Brimelow, Peter. 1995. *Alien Nation: Common Sense About America's Immigration Disaster*. New York: Random House.

Bullard, Robert, ed. 1994. *Unequal Protection: Environmental Justice and Communities of Color*. San Francisco: Sierra Club Books.

———, ed. 1993. *Confronting Environmental Racism: Voices from the Grassroots*. Boston: South End Press.

Bullard, Robert D., Glenn S. Johnson, and Angel O. Torres. 2000. "Environmental Costs and Consequences of Sprawl." In *Sprawl City: Race, Politics, and Planning in Atlanta*. Washington, DC: Island Press.

Chapple, Karen, Matthew Zook, Radhika Kunamneni, AnnaLee Saxenian, Steven Weber, and Beverly Crawford. 2000. *From Promising Practices to Promising Futures: Job Training and Information Technology for Disadvantaged Adults*. San Francisco: Bay Area Video Coalition.

Dorfman, Lori and Vincent Schiraldi. 2001. *Off Balance: Youth, Race & Crime in the News*. Report from Building Blocks for Youth (www.buildingblocksforyouth.org).

Dreher, George F., and Taylor H. Cox, Jr. 2000. "Labor Market Mobility and Cash Compensation: The Moderating Effects of Race and Gender." *Academy of Management Journal*, Vol. 43, No. 5.

Fix, Michael, and Wendy Zimmerman. 2000. "The Integration of Immigrant Families in the United States." The Citizen's Commission for Civil Rights Biennial Report on Federal Civil Rights and Enforcement.

Grogan, Paul S., and Tony Proscio. 2000. *Comeback Cities: A Blueprint for Urban Neighborhood Revival*. Boulder, CO: Westview Press.

Haycock, Kati. 1998. "Good Teaching Matters . . . A Lot." *Thinking K-16*, Vol. 3, No 2. A publication of The Education Trust. Summer.

Hum, Tarry, and Michaela Zonta. 2000. "Residential Patterns of Asian Pacific Americans." In Paul M. Ong, ed. *The State of Asian Pacific America: Transforming Race Relations*. Los Angeles, CA: Leadership Education for Asian Pacifics, Inc., Asian Pacific American Public Policy Institute, and UCLA Asian American Studies Center.

Jencks, Christopher, and Meredith Phillips. 1998. "America's Next Achievement Test: Closing the Black-White Test Score Gap." *American Prospect*, Vol. 9, No. 40.

Katz, Bruce, ed. 2000. *Reflections on Regionalism*. Washington, DC: Brookings Institution Press.

Lester, James P., David W. Allen, and Kelly M. Hill. 2001. *Environmental Injustice in the United States: Myths and Realities*. Boulder, CO: Westview Press.

Li, Wei. 1999. "The Emergence and Manifestation of the Chinese Ethnoburb in Los Angeles' San Gabriel Valley." *Journal of Asian American Studies*, Vol. 2, No. 1.

Marable, Manning. 2000. "Facing the Demon Head On: Institutional Racism and the Prison Industrial Complex." *Southern Changes*, Vol. 22, No. 3. Fall.

Morello-Frosch, Rachel. 1997. "Environmental Justice and California's 'Riskscape': The Distribution of Air Toxics and Associated Cancer and Non-Cancer Risks Among Diverse Communities." Dissertation. Environmental Health Sciences, UC Berkeley.

Morello-Frosch, Rachel, Manuel Pastor, Jr., and James Sadd. 2001. "Environmental Justice and Southern California's 'Riskscape': The Distribution of Air Toxics Exposures and Health Risks Among Diverse Communities." *Urban Affairs Review*.

Nasser, Haya El. 2001. "Minorities reshape suburbs"; "Minorities make choice to live with their own." *USA Today*, July 9.

National Telecommunications and Information Administration (NTIA). 1999. *Falling Through the Net: Defining the Digital Divide*. See www.ntia.doc.gov/ntiahome/fttn99/FTTN.pdf.

Nelson, Marla K., and Lisa J. Servon. 2001. "Why Planners Should Work to Close the Digital Divide." Submitted to the *Journal of the American Planning Association*.

Orfield, Myron. 1997. *Metropolitics: A Regional Agenda for Community and Stability*. Washington, DC: Brookings Institution Press.

Pastor, Jr., Manuel. 2001. "Geography and Opportunity." In Neil Smelser, William Julius Wilson, Faith Mitchell, eds. *America Becoming: Racial Trends and Their Consequences*, Volume 1, National Research Council Commission on Behavioral and Social Sciences and Education. Washington, DC: National Academy Press.

Pastor, Jr., Manuel, James Sadd, and John Hipp, 2001. "Which Came First? Toxic Facilities, Minority Move-in, and Environmental Justice." *Journal of Urban Affairs*, Vol. 23, No. 1.

Pastor, Jr., Manuel, Peter Dreier, Eugene Grigsby, and Marta Lopez-Garza. 2000. *Regions That Work: How Cities and Suburbs Can Grow Together.* Minneapolis, MN: University of Minnesota Press.

Peirce, Neal R., with Curtis W. Johnson and John Stuart Hall. 1993. *Citistates: How Urban America Can Prosper in a Competitive World.* Washington, DC: Seven Locks Press.

Poe-Yamagata, Eileen, and Michael A. Jones. 2000. *And Justice for Some.* Report from Building Blocks for Youth (www.buildingblocksforyouth.org).

PolicyLink. 2001(a). *Bridging the Organizational Divide: Toward a Comprehensive Approach to the Digital Divide.* Oakland, CA: PolicyLink.

———. 2001(b). *Community-Centered Policing: A Force for Change.* Oakland, CA: PolicyLink.

———. 2000. *From Promising Practices to Promising Futures: Job Training in Information Technology for Disadvantaged Adults (Synthesis of Key Findings).* Oakland, CA: PolicyLink.

Robyn, Linda, and David E. Camacho. 1998. "*Bishigendan Akii:* Respect the Earth." In David E. Camacho, ed. *Environmental Injustices, Political Struggles: Race, Class, and the Environment.* Durham, NC: Duke University Press.

Saito, Leland. 1998. *Race and Politics: Asian Americans, Latinos, and Whites in a Los Angeles Suburb.* Urbana, IL: University of Illinois Press.

Savitch, H.B., David Collins, Daniel Sanders, and John Markham. 1993. "Ties That Bind: Central Cities, Suburbs, and the New Metropolitan Region." *Economic Development Quarterly,* Vol. 7, No. 4.

Saxenian, AnnaLee. 1999. *Silicon Valley's New Immigrant Entrepreneurs.* San Francisco: Public Policy Institute of California.

Skocpol, Theda. 1991. "Targeting Within Universalism: Politically Viable Policies to Combat Poverty in the United States." In Christopher Jencks and Paul E. Peterson, eds. *The Urban Underclass.* Washington, DC: Brookings Institution Press.

Steele, Claude M., and Joshua Aronson. 1995. "Stereotype Threat and the Intellectual Test Performance of African-Americans." *Journal of Personality and Social Psychology,* Vol. 69, No. 5.

Tseng, Thomas. 2001. "Ethnicity in the Electronic Age: Looking at the Internet Through Multicultural Lens." Report, Cultural Access Group, Access Worldwide Communications.

Wilson, William Julius. 1999. *The Bridge over the Racial Divide: Rising Inequality and Coalition Politics.* Berkeley, CA: University of California Press.

Zielbauer, Paul. 2001. "Felons Gain Voting Rights in Connecticut." *New York Times,* May 14.

6

New Leadership
for the 21st Century

The challenges and opportunities on the road ahead call for a new type of leadership. Significant progress has been made, especially since the social justice movements of the 1960s and 1970s, when strong leadership decisions expanded opportunity for all. Leaders from various sectors—government, religious, labor, education, the media, community, and business—continue to give meaning and weight to the hard-fought victories. The leadership necessary was bold, focused, and supported by mass movements and loyal constituencies. The question is whether 21st-century realities can be confronted without rethinking or updating how today's leaders operate and interact with each other.

Before forecasting new leadership skill requirements, we examine the past and current crop of leaders and from whence they came. Consider the following historical thumbnails.

Religious leaders—black and white—played a seminal role in the civil rights movement from the 1960s on. Without dynamic leaders—best represented by Dr. Martin

Luther King, Jr., Rev. (later Congressman and Ambassador) Andrew Young, and Rev. Wyatt Tee Walker—who mobilized grassroots communities, forged successful coalitions, and launched peaceful protests, the racial inequities of this country would never have gained national attention; landmark civil rights legislation would never have been enacted.

From community development corporations (CDCs) to health clinics, many of the gains of the past two decades are directly attributable to local, grassroots leaders creatively solving problems. CDCs, in particular, were in the vanguard of community revitalization efforts in the 1960s and continue to be a force for change. These neighborhood based nonprofit organizations—small, nimble, and intensely local—grew under the visionary leadership of foundation executives such as Franklin Thomas of the Ford Foundation. Strong CDC leaders, such as Gonza Twitty who headed up one of the original twenty-two CDCs in the South and Dan Maxwell, past president of the CDC of Kansas City—one of the oldest in the country—emerged out of communities of color. Other grassroots leaders such as Ernesto Cortes of the Industrial Areas Foundation in Texas and Gloria Molina, the first Latina county supervisor in Los Angeles County, have been instrumental in championing social justice causes that benefit communities of color.

While grassroots leaders are largely responsible for bringing the discourse about racial inequality to the national spotlight, political leaders as prominent as President Lyndon B. Johnson provided structural remedies against legalized discrimination through such laws as the Civil Rights Act of 1964, the Voting Rights Act of 1965, followed shortly by the Fair Housing Act, as we discussed in chapter 4. On Capitol Hill, a handful of black members of Congress wielded far more clout than their numbers suggested: Adam Clayton Powell, Jr. and Shirley Chisholm of New York, Charles Diggs and John Conyers of Detroit, and Gus Hawkins of Los Angeles, to name a few. They united to found the Congressional Black Caucus in 1969. A decade

later, Herman Badillo of New York, Kika de la Garza and
Henry Gonzalez of Texas, Manuel Lujan of New Mexico,
and Ed Roybal of California became the founding members
of the Congressional Hispanic Caucus. The members of
both caucuses were among the visionary men and women
who voiced the needs and concerns of underrepresented
and disenfranchised people of color on national and international levels. In the late 1980s, Representatives Norm
Mineta and Robert Matsui and Senator Daniel Inouye,
among others, led the successful effort for redress and
reparations for Japanese Americans who were unjustifiably
interned in World War II.

The world of commerce had its leaders—both minority
and nonminority—promoting social justice and inclusiveness through successful affirmative action and diversity
programs. Decades before Kenneth Chenault was in the
executive suites at American Express, Roy Wilkins of the
NAACP, Vernon Jordan of the National Urban League, and
Dr. Dorothy I. Height of the National Council of Negro
Women laid the foundation for greater inclusion in the corporate world. Minority subcontracting, recruiting minority
candidates, and training and outreach programs geared to
minorities have promoted equal opportunity in hiring and
advancements (see Box 6-1).

Labor leaders such as Cesar Chavez, Dolores Huerta, A.
Philip Randolph, and Philip VeraCruz must be credited for
their tremendous achievements as well in helping to reduce
the income disparities among racial groups. Most recently,
the AFL-CIO, as we discussed in the section entitled
"Immigrant Policy" in chapter 5, has been responsible for
galvanizing immigrant workers to assert their rights to a living wage and fair benefits.

21st-Century Trends

As we have argued throughout *Searching for the Uncommon
Common Ground*, this very young century is already usher-
ing its unique challenges to the forefront. Those who

Box 6-1. Business Profits from Promoting Racial Justice and Inclusiveness

In the corporate world, the promotion of inclusiveness is evident in a company's approaches to recruiting, hiring, and retaining a diverse workforce. Financial success and effective diversity programs are closely linked as several studies have shown. Covenant Investment Management conducted a study in 1993 that showed that the 100 companies with the best equal-employment practices had five-year annualized returns of 18.3 percent, while the 100 firms with the worst practices had returns of only 7.9 percent (Business for Social Responsibility, 2000).

Diversity efforts through purchasing from minority owned and operated companies have proven to be successful for Ford Motor Company. In 2000, it was the largest purchaser of goods and services from minority owned and operated companies among U.S. corporations. Steve Larson, manager, Minority Supplier Development at Ford, stated, "It's good business. Minority suppliers provide Ford with some of the highest quality and competitively priced goods and services. . . . With the U.S. minority population nearing 30 percent, it is in our best long-term interest to invest in minority businesses and communities. These are our customers" (Weiser and Zadek, 2000).

Indirect benefits, not always quantifiable, have led to increased profitability as well. For example, anecdotal evidence from several companies—Dupont and Intel among them—showed that a more diverse workforce improves productivity. Reduced turnover was another benefit. A 1997 study by the Families & Work Institute found that employees in supportive environments with respect to issues such as equal opportunities for advancement and lack of discrimination were most satisfied with their jobs (Business for Social Responsibility, 2000).

The substantial financial and nonmonetary benefits to workforce diversity and to the development of diverse markets have not been ignored by successful managers. More than eight out of ten Fortune 500 respondents to a 1998 survey said their top-level executives think diversity management is either very important, important, or somewhat important (Business for Social Responsibility, 2000).

aspire to lead must prepare themselves to deal with a stew of complex issues that will confront them, based on some emerging trends not faced by their predecessors. To quote the mantra of civil rights activist Jesse Jackson, Sr.: "You can't teach what you don't know; you can't lead where you don't go."

The 21st-century leaders will have to develop techniques and strategies that will allow successful anticipation of and maneuvering through several trends that appear on the horizon.

Chief among these trends is the so-called browning of America, or what we refer to in chapter 1 as the "changing" America, and the array of issues affiliated with the rapid demographic shifts in cities, suburbs, and rural areas. The experience in California is instructive. Many areas such as South Central Los Angeles have experienced a surge in Latino immigrant populations where African Americans had been the majority. The challenge to churches and other institutions that have long served the needs of African American communities is whether they can also serve the diverse and sometimes conflicting needs of immigrant populations. They, along with other community leaders, will have to assist in reconciling differences among groups. A key requirement for any 21st-century leader is to orchestrate these groups so that they will work together for their common good, to foster community goodwill, and to build infrastructure and programs that will improve everyone's standard of living and generate neighborhood vitality.

Another trend of paramount importance is the interconnectedness of issues and their solutions. Today's society presents a modern day "chicken-or-egg" syndrome. For example, educational achievement is linked not only to teacher and parental involvement, but also to improving community conditions such as reducing violence and increasing access to health care. Also consider: it would be short-sighted to create jobs without examining unequal educational opportunities and the lack of efficient public transportation. As issues become increasingly complex and intertwined, isolating a single solution to an individual problem becomes virtually impossible. To challenge racial and economic disparities, leaders must understand this complexity, articulate integrated visions, and strategize accordingly.

The changing electorate is another challenging trend. Up to one-third of the voting population refuses to affiliate with either major national party. These independents vote according to issues, not party affiliation. Given their growing ranks and the polarization of the two major parties—a chasm grown even wider in the aftermath of the 2000 presidential election in which thousands of Florida's African American citizens were disenfranchised—political leaders are hard pressed to garner widespread support for measures that address racial inequality. At a time of unparalleled relative prosperity and power for the United States on a global scale, it is regrettable that few leaders on the national political scene hold themselves accountable for eliminating racial disparities. The next generation of leaders will be required to mobilize for the type of programs and principles advanced in *Searching for the Uncommon Common Ground*. They will also need to redefine the terms of the debate, working with the media to their mutual advantage. Their charge will include restoring the moral, ethical, and empowering vision of racial justice that fueled the civil rights movement and that harvested the legislative victories that most Americans—of all colors and persuasions—enjoy the fruits of today. The stakes are high.

The fourth trend is the present superheated economy, which has an indirect impact on racial justice efforts. Today's extremely competitive market exacerbates the tendency of corporations to focus on short-term profits and stock prices, instead of issues that create long-term benefits such as practices that value and foster inclusiveness. In the business arena, workforce diversity has advanced considerably; outreach to previously ignored markets is also on the upswing. Will these progressive movements last? Diversity practices could be implemented because of the need to comply with the law rather than becoming deeply ingrained in the corporate conscience. Furthermore, businesses constantly oriented to the short term will be reluctant to shift gears to consider markets that are unfamiliar to them.

Looking beyond one's immediate sphere is a must in this new century: globalization has enormous implications for all leaders who are working toward racial justice. The political backlash against globalization has led not only to civic protests but also to debate about how to make international institutions more accountable. As economies across the world become increasingly interconnected, leaders must expand their global vision and understanding. For example, garment workers—largely people of color—are among the working poor in the United States in part because they are competing with even more poorly paid workers in other countries. Leaders will be unable to effect and improve the working and health conditions of garment workers without a global understanding of change in this industry.

In an article written for The California Endowment, Deborah Meehan (1999) highlighted the work of a team from the Center for the Advanced Study of Leadership.

"This team identified several significant trends and leadership implications. They suggest that 21st-century leaders must be prepared to understand and lead under conditions of globalization, increasing stress on the environment, increasing speed and dissemination of information technology, growing diversity, rapid change, unprecedented complexity, increasing interdependence, and an ever-widening gap between the haves and have-nots." These implications are not only applicable for a small elite, but for all levels of leadership across sectors.

Barriers to Effective Leadership

In addition to the new challenges rooted in macroscopic trends that are seen in the 21st century, there are several barriers—self-imposed as well as structural or practical—that leaders must overcome in order to effectively advance a racial justice agenda. These barriers are not insurmountable, and the debate on what is needed to develop new leadership is beginning to spread in nonprofit, business, and political circles.

Perhaps the biggest barrier to effective leadership in the area of racial equality is the American population's overall disengagement from issues of national and local importance. Americans' lack of engagement is evident in declining voter participation rates, in the reduced amount of civic participation, and in the general cynicism about government and politics. Far too many people avoid the subject of race altogether, whether fearful of being criticized or blamed for historical atrocities, or—as is often the case—oblivious to racial problems. Leaders must again rise to the challenge of bringing racial justice issues to the forefront. U.S. democracy requires government by elected officials who are accountable to all the people. It is in America's best interest that everyone be engaged in securing racial justice for all.

Failure to engage in substantive discussion and action leads to governmental paralysis and gridlock in matters of legislation, policy, and program implementation. The nation is polarized as to whether racial inequality even exists. Some believe that past civil rights advancements leveled the playing field, race-conscious remedies for discrimination are therefore unnecessary, and individual responsibility is key to improving one's social and economic status. At the other end of the spectrum are those who see a very uneven playing field and thus demand societal accountability to ensure racial equality. They believe that structural racism must be eliminated and race-conscious measures must be implemented if necessary. These polarized views are no excuse for stagnation.

Common ground can be reached when approached creatively, for example, when personal experiences with race are used proactively. When Representative Dan Ponder (a white Republican from what he called an "ultraconservative" rural district) rose to speak moments after the Georgia State House voted 83–82 to shelve a proposal to make crimes carry tougher penalties when they are motivated by hatred, he gave the speech herein (Roddy, 2000; See Box 6-2).

Republicans and Democrats alike gave Ponder two standing ovations and then outlawed all hate crimes by a vote of 116–49. Georgia Governor Roy Barnes signed the new law at a synagogue scarred by swastikas.

Achieving common ground is difficult, even among those who believe that significant structural barriers that stifle individual efforts still remain. All too often, different and sometimes competing agendas exist among groups that are separated by race, ethnicity, geography, political view, or "turf." Groups are often divided over their goals and approaches based on ethnic group affiliation; intragroup tensions cloud the vision, for example, among ethnic groups within the Asian Pacific Islander community.

One reason these divisions thrive is the absence of a clear, focused vision for racial justice. In the 1960s and 1970s, the unquestioned goal was ending legalized discrimination. Leaders from all walks of life recognized the need

Box 6-2. The Speech That Turned Heads

On March 16, [2000,] a proponent of hate crimes legislation rose [in the Georgia state legislature] to speak both
his mind and his heart in a moment that transcended
politics.

When Georgia's hate crimes bill was about to be tabled
into oblivion, Representative Dan Ponder, Jr., asked to
address the assembly, where he spoke of both the memory of his youth and the conscience of his manhood.

Nine of Ponder's great-great-grandfathers fought for the
Confederacy. Several owned slaves. He had not one
ancestor born north of the Mason-Dixon Line. His bona
fides firmly established, he told the story of the family
employee who raised him. Her name was Mary Ward.
She was black.

"She began working for my family before I was born,"
Ponder said. Her grandmother had raised Ponder's
mother. The Ponder children called Mary "May-Mar."
She traveled with the family on its vacations in Florida.
She taught him to play ball. She read to him. She raised
him as she would her own children.

"One day, when I was about twelve or thirteen I was
leaving for school. As I was walking out the door, she
turned to kiss me goodbye. And for some reason, I
turned my head. She stopped and looked at me with a
look that absolutely burns in my memory right now and
she said, 'You didn't kiss me because I'm black.'"

She was right. Young Dan Ponder denied it. He made
his excuses, but he knew. Raised in a place and time
when his own father insisted on paying his black employees the same as whites but who kept separate water foun-
tains and eating tables in his factory cafeteria, Dan
Ponder knew why he wasn't kissing this woman who
loved him unconditionally and without artifice.

"I have lived with the shame and memory of my betrayal of Mary Ward's love for me," Ponder told his colleagues.

He remembered his shame the day he'd turned his face away from one who loved him as her own. He remembered two decades ago when he traveled back to Alabama to help bury May-Mar. He remembered it and promised himself someday, somehow, he would redeem his moment of dishonor.

So, on the morning of March 16, without telling his wife he planned to do it, Dan Ponder, Jr., conservative Republican, stood in the well of the Georgia House and told the kind of story no politician is ever supposed to tell on himself.

"Hate is all around us," Ponder said. "And it takes shape and form in ways that are somehow so small that we don't even recognize them to begin with, until they somehow become acceptable to us."

The bill, he acknowledged, might be a legal futility. Ponder is not a lawyer. But this was bigger than law.

"I don't really care that anyone is ever prosecuted under this bill," Ponder said. "But I do care that we take this moment, this time in history, to say that we are going to send a message."

to advocate for laws that created equal opportunity, guaranteed equal rights, and afforded equal access. Today no across-the-board racial justice agenda that includes specific goals exists.

Related to this lack of vision is widespread fragmentation that is evident in various forms. After the Los Angeles riots in 1992, the MultiCultural Collaborative (MCC) wrote a comprehensive assessment of human relations conflicts. In *Race, Power, and Promise in Los Angeles*, MCC disclosed that at the moment when Los Angeles's diverse communities (from the grassroots to the mainstream) most needed to work together to address the institutional causes of poverty and tension, the city's leadership was becoming more polarized (Choi et al., 1996). Institutional responses to human and race relations were fragmented and crisis-driven, often not linked to the social and economic causes that were at the root of many intergroup and racial conflicts. While it has been analyzed from many different angles—including economic despair, outrage over the criminal justice system, and intensifying interracial conflicts—the failure of leadership that the Multi-Cultural Collaborative described was not unique to Los Angeles.

New Leadership Defined

In light of the emerging trends and possible barriers that leaders face in the new millennium, the nature of leadership itself needs to be qualitatively different. A leader in the 21st century should be a problem solver, a life-long learner, and an ethical example for others. To lead, one should have a penchant for action as well as a commitment to reflection and reassessment and be able to collaborate with others. There are four specific dimensions that we next highlight: (1) a commitment to racial justice, (2) the embracing of a multiracial perspective, (3) the ability to make cross-sector linkages, and (4) a commitment to acquiring and improving skills.

A Commitment to Racial Justice and Equality

A requisite quality of the leadership for this new millennium is an underlying moral and ethical commitment to racial justice that informs leaders' actions. We understand that leaders have multiple commitments and are often committed to issues they identify with irrespective of gender, class, sexual orientation, age, or religion. Yet we highlight the need for a commitment to racial justice because the real-life consequences of racial disparities in every aspect of American life cannot be ignored.

Furthermore, leaders must be fully devoted to eliminating racial disparities because of the growing threat to programs, initiatives, and efforts that stemmed from the civil rights movement. Some think racism will evaporate over time as a result of generational change and better education. We believe, however, that racial attitudes may soften over time, but the structural inequality will not evaporate if left uncorrected. Therefore, it is urgent for all leaders to strive to reduce racial disparities and foster a commitment to full inclusion through dialogue, understanding, and action.

A Multiethnic and Multiracial Perspective

Leaders must be multiethnic and multiracial in perspective. They should lead according to principles and policies that have a positive impact on more than an individual racial or ethnic subgroup. The James Irvine Foundation has described such leaders as "border bridgers" who must speak to and for their constituents while earning the respect of the constituents of others, as Craig McGarvey, a program officer at the foundation, explained to Stewart Kwoh in an interview in January 2001. Border bridgers are leaders who "move with integrity outside their own circles, always seeking a circle that is broader. They find common ground by setting difference aside and focusing on interests that can be shared."

The growing racial diversity of the United States in general, and many poor neighborhoods in particular, requires that leaders have both a universal concern for all disadvantaged people as well as an understanding of particular groups' specific needs. These dual—and sometimes dueling—concerns may lead to situations where leaders must negotiate how best to bring groups that are in conflict over significant issues together as well as to mitigate disputes over competition for limited resources.

For instance, during the debate over Proposition 187—the California ballot initiative that promised to deny welfare benefits, education, and health and other social services to undocumented immigrants—the proponents of the initiative pitted minority groups against each other. Fanning the tenuous, underlying conflict that already existed between African Americans and Latinos, proponents argued that immigrants stole jobs from low-income Americans and overwhelmed an already overly burdened social and health service system. African American and other leaders were challenged to show their own constituents that the immigrant struggles were similar to their own experiences and that a pro-immigrant agenda supporting services to undocumented people would preserve the civil rights of all Californians.

Leaders in the new millennium must possess multiracial/multiethnic perspective that fully appreciates each group's needs while successfully advocating for multigroup goals that produce a greater good for everyone.

The Ability to Make Cross-Sector Linkages

While there is an understandable tendency to focus exclusively in one's own terrain, on one's own issue, or in one's own racial or ethnic group, such isolation can detract from creating a larger impact and derail efforts at broader coalition building. "Historical separation, the artificial parsing of social issues along racial lines, and an absence of communication and trusting relationships among activists in different fields frustrate the development of synergistic efforts," as Dayna Cunningham, a program officer at the Rockefeller Foundation, stated to Stewart Kwoh in an interview in March 2001. "Rather than joint strategies to tackle major problems in multidisciplinary ways, problem-solving efforts remain fragmented, disparate, and weaker than they need to be."

These inhibitors are present in the corporate world as

well. Today's captains of industry must be able to move beyond the traditional top-down leadership approach to a more horizontal, collaborative style that has the advantage of being quicker and more inclusive, utilizing diverse ideas and interests to take advantage of opportunities. At the same time, in light of today's economy, they need to deal with the intersection of domestic and global forces. In the context of working for racial justice, collaborative leadership can ensure that the table is inclusive, that developing leadership occurs at all levels of organizations in order to tap the full potential of every individual, and that coalitions can more effectively emerge.

A Commitment to Improving Skills

Finally, leaders must constantly acquire new, and improve existing, skills. To fully understand their terrain, leaders should pursue a wide range of information sources, including experts—both in the academy and in the field—formal training, and peer learning. Understanding the implications of the global economy does not come from local experience alone; grasping how systems function—and malfunction—requires broader study. Computer and media literacy also require study.

The ability to collaborate is a learned skill, and although collaborations among different sectors and even among peers are often difficult, they provide a scale and learning that go-it-alone approaches simply cannot allow. In the final analysis, such skills are tested in the cauldron of getting initiatives passed by electoral bodies, creating and implementing programs to address injustices, and mobilizing for positive changes for communities and groups.

Approaches to Developing Effective Leadership

Effective leadership requires support from and interaction with peers, mentors, and coaches. In this section we high-

light leadership networks, leadership development programs, and ongoing leadership development within organizing campaigns, legal cases, and institutions. Many
time-proven ways to develop leadership already exist.
While we focus on three approaches, they are by no means
exhaustive. For example, mentoring has long been one of
the most direct ways of developing leaders. Through this
type of relationship, one can develop important leadership
qualities and often ascend to the leader's position. We do,
however, believe that the following approaches may be the
most accessible and scalable.

Leadership Networks

An important approach that builds and nurtures existing
or emerging leaders is the formation of networks, particularly among those who are similarly committed to racial
equality and inclusion. These networks should be multiracial and cross-sectoral, including nonprofit, business, religious, and academic leaders. Ethnic-specific networks,
however, can play a positive role. The latter should be forward looking in addition to being responsive to immediate
issues.

Ideally, multiracial networks need to be in place before
crises occur so that trusting relationships can be established. Relationship building is key: it can be the base from
which true coalitions are built and new solutions developed. These networks can also form crucial channels of
communication, not just dialogue or study circles. The
multiracial character of these networks should not preempt
ethnic-specific networks or avoid ethnic- or racial-specific
issues. Having several leadership circles or networks is
important.

Experiments are ongoing in building cross-sector networks in key social movements. For example, the Rockefeller Foundation has developed a leadership program to
allow civil rights, environmental, community building, and
labor leaders to build a network to explore overlapping

interests and influence each other's work. In addition to building trusting relationships, investigating large-scale trends across sectors, permitting exploration of shared interests and obstacles to collaboration, and enabling ongoing communication of ideas, joint projects have been developed that model effective problem solving on specific race related policy issues and foster collaboration among leaders from segmented social change movements.

An example of a leadership network is the Digital Steppingstones (DSS) project, launched by the Tomás Rivera Policy Institute (Pachon et al., 2000). The DSS project is investigating how access to advanced technologies in low-income and minority communities can best be achieved. Collaborating with knowledgeable librarians, educators, and community members, this issue based leadership network has produced major policy recommendations through its research and findings that address the need to encourage partnerships between corporate sectors and public access centers. The recommendations also address the need to optimize resources by promoting cooperation among public access centers. This network has allowed member collaborators to avoid reinventing the wheel and to learn important lessons from each other in order to take a lead in reducing the digital divide in their communities.

With eighteen prominent leaders from business, academia, labor, and the media, the Business Enterprise Trust was an active business leadership network for seven years. A national nonprofit organization, it sought to identify bold, creative leadership that incorporated a commitment to social justice and community as a pivotal part of its vision for business. These businesses, once identified, were upheld as exemplary, brought into the national spotlight by the network, and served as positive corporate responsibility models.

Business leaders have also fostered networks to confront racism directly. Project Change, first established in 1991 by Levi Strauss & Co. through its corporate foundation, builds local networks in four cities to address racial prejudice and institutional racism. Networks or task forces are created, and after an assessment of institutional racism, business, community, and other partners work on projects to alleviate such barriers and provide training in areas such as fair lending, hate crimes prevention, educational advancement, and improved law enforcement.

Collaborations of foundations are rare in cities. In the aftermath of the Los Angeles riots, however, over twenty-five foundations networked to create the Los Angeles Urban Funders to build leadership capacity and community revitalization efforts in three impoverished neighborhoods. Not only have the neighborhoods developed stronger leaders, but the foundations have gained valuable knowledge and insight from community partners and other foundations. Plans are underway to expand to other neighborhoods and to share the foundations' lessons nationally.

Leadership Development Programs

An abundance of literature on leadership development programs exists (see, for example, Meehan, 1999, and Campbell and Associates, 1997). Such programs can contribute significantly in developing skills, experience, networks, and personal relationships that strengthen the leadership capacity of individuals and organizations.

While we are not experts on leadership development programs, we do have a few observations. First, leadership development programs in any setting must deal with race and cultural awareness as a clear focus. Searching for common ground is important; alienating participants by exclusively focusing on racial differences is not productive. Yet race issues will surface or resurface, so it is better to plan for this discussion. John Maguire and colleagues emphasize this point in "15 Tools for Creating Healthy, Productive Interracial/Multicultural Communities—A Community Builder's Tool Kit" (Maguire et al., 2000).

The time spent at the beginning [either of a community building project or leadership training program, according to John Maguire] working on race will be well-repaid later. When you avoid this painful, protracted conversation at the outset, proposed partnerships fall apart, leading to head-shaking—and sometimes fingerpointing—over the intractability associated with race and the depth of animosities held by one group in relation to another.

The more leadership development programs deal with real situations and practical collaborations, the more likely it is that they will have a positive impact on participants' daily work and lives. The Leadership Development in Interethnic Relations program, cosponsored by the Asian Pacific American Legal Center, the Southern Christian Leadership Conference, and the Central American Resource Center, consists of three components in the six-month training class for adults and high school students: cultural awareness training, including personal, cultural, racial, and ethnic backgrounds and the role of stereotypes; skills building, including conflict resolution, team building, and violence prevention; and a community project completed in multiethnic teams working with local community leaders. It is this last component—the community project—that most tests collaboration skills. The bonds and trust resulting from these projects usually last well beyond the program.

In its examination of leadership development programs for youth that emphasize racial justice issues, the MultiCultural Collaborative (2001) found that practical involvement is a key component of effective programs. At the same time, it learned that successful programs also provide training and analysis of the larger causes and systems so that youth participants can understand their personal experiences in the context of broader societal trends and issues.

Finally, we agree with Meehan (1999) when she writes:

Unusual partnerships and strategic alliances within the community have catalyzed the most innovative and successful community revitalization and development initiatives. An understanding of the 21st century leadership challenges of globalization, disparities of wealth, complexity, interconnected systems, change, and diversity all call for strong cross-sectoral collaborations and solutions. Surprisingly, there are few established leadership development programs to foster the development of these teams. Business and civic leaders rarely sit at the table with grassroots community leaders engaged in collective problem-solving.

Support for the varied leadership development programs, particularly those that have impact on racial justice, should be enhanced and expanded. Businesses need to be challenged to see these leadership development efforts as part of their corporate responsibility commitment and as a preferred way to do business. Competitive pressures have led to decreasing support for measures to address racial disparities both within companies and within communities, and yet the success of most businesses depends on the vitality of the communities in which their customers live.

Some foundations have also taken a new or renewed interest in leadership development and organizational capacity building. For example, the California Wellness Foundation has significantly increased core operating support grants to build the capacity of nonprofit organizations and the leadership of those organizations. This kind of grantmaking acknowledges the importance of strengthening their partners rather than focusing only on program grants. Foundations such as the Ford Foundation have recently initiated leadership development programs to highlight the contributions of new leaders to community revitalization in many fields.

Ongoing Leadership Development

Leadership comes from many sources. It should not be limited to leadership networks and leadership development programs. Mentoring has traditionally been a rudimentary way to develop leadership. What is essential is an ongoing commitment to develop leadership as an integral component of achieving racial justice. Training may occur within organizations: it may arise during an organizing drive, may be required during a civil rights lawsuit, or may happen as part of regular interactions in business. Opportunities for leadership development are everywhere.

A case in point: during the civil rights lawsuit against the El Monte contractors—manufacturers and retailers who were responsible for the enslavement of more than seventy Thai American garment workers in a sweatshop in southern California—the garment workers themselves were educated and trained to become their own leaders, to speak out against exploitation in their industry. The case was complicated by the fact that there were over twenty Latino workers in a front shop where workers were not enslaved but certainly were exploited. Hundreds of hours of discussion, training, and nurturing led to many of the workers speaking at rallies and at the California legislature in behalf of stronger anti-sweatshop laws.

Penda Hair (2001) lifts up the emerging field of racial justice innovation as communities work with lawyers using a range of tools to challenge exclusion based on race and ethnicity. In the process, these advocates are buttressing local leadership and reinvigorating local democracy.

One case from Boston illustrates this practice. In 1993, when the city proposed developing a parking garage on one of Chinatown's last parcels of underdeveloped land, a coalition of residents and activists rallied to stop it. Taking democratic decision making as its core principle, the coalition launched a relentless organizing campaign against approval of the garage. Teaming with a group of young legal service lawyers, the coalition mobilized residents for administrative hearings, conducted a community-wide referendum, and held news conferences and cultural events to stimulate public involvement among marginalized immigrant groups. The coalition made leadership development a priority. Activities organized by resident committees created repeat opportunities to develop public speaking skills, learn community outreach, communicate messages, and engage neighbors. In the process, the coalition opened the neighborhood's decision making and won a decisive victory to preserve community open space.

Even with limited resources, nonprofits and others can advance staff and board development through a number of approaches that promote crossracial and cross-sector organizational exchanges to share information and lessons. In addition, organizations can plan office training to understand other communities and their infrastructures so that connections can be made easier in the course of their work and activities. Leadership development, especially concerning racial justice issues, must be ongoing.

Conclusion

Given the challenges of America's evolving demographic landscape and the multitude of pressing social issues, 21st-century leadership must focus on racial justice and the elimination of disparities. Without this commitment to and vision of equality across all sectors—political, religious, business, grassroots, labor, education, media, and government—the nation will not thrive. These new leaders need multiple perspectives, and the initiative to work collaboratively with individuals in different fields with different experiences and perspectives. Creative leadership programs can teach and spread these skills to men and women who will boldly assert a moral vision for equality and provide pragmatic strategies to realize that vision.

References

Business for Social Responsibility. 2000. "Diversity." www.bsr.org/resourcecenter.

Campbell and Associates. 1997. "Lessons Learned About Grassroots Community Leadership." Report commissioned by the Kellogg Foundation.

Choi, Cindy, Ruben Lizardo, and Gary Phillips. 1996. *Race, Power, and*

Promise in Los Angeles: An Assessment of Responses to Human Relations Conflict. Los Angeles, CA: MultiCultural Collaborative.

Hair, Penda D. 2001. *Louder Than Words: Lawyers, Communities and the Struggle for Justice.* New York: The Rockefeller Foundation.

Maguire, John, Sally Leiderman, and John Egerton. 2000. "A Community Builder's Tool Kit—15 Tools for Creating Healthy, Productive, Interracial/Multicultural Communities." Claremont, CA: The Institute for Democratic Renewal and The Project Change Anti-Racism Initiative.

Meehan, Deborah. 1999. "Leadership Development Opportunities and Challenges: A Scan of the Field of the Leadership Literature and the Field of Leadership Development." Woodland Hills, CA: The California Endowment.

MultiCultural Collaborative. 2001. "The Future of Change." Los Angeles, CA: MultiCultural Collaborative.

Pachon, Harry P., Elsa E. Macias, and Paula Y. Bagasao. 2000. "Minority Access to Information Technology: Lessons Learned" (Occasional Paper N. 67, Latino Studies Series). East Lansing, MI: Michigan State University, Julian Samora Research Institute.

Roddy, Dennis. 2000. An adaptation of "The Speech That Turned Heads." *Pittsburgh Post-Gazette*, June 24.

Weiser, John, and Simon Zadek. 2000. "Conversations with Disbelievers: Persuading Companies to Address Social Changes." New York: The Ford Foundation.

7

A Vision for Action

The magnitude of the challenges presented by race cannot be underestimated. To make progress, the entire culture around racial discourse will need to shift. The nation must first acknowledge that a problem still exists— an American problem, not mere complaints from special interest groups. A dialogue about race is needed that is less emotionally confrontational, more fully informed and rigorously pursued. No effort can be successful unless all participants make a real effort to understand the experiences of others whose points of view differ from their own. The nation must commit to a course of action that is purposeful and based on sound policy that embraces its diversity and works to achieve economic and social equity.

Accepting these challenges, *Searching for the Uncommon Common Ground* attempts to set a context for productive dialogue that can lead to viable public policy. At the outset, we identified five dimensions in the debate on race: *the black-white paradigm versus multiculturalism, diversity versus racial and social justice, universal versus particular strategies, national versus local responsibility*, and *structural factors versus individual initiative*. Out of context, it may appear that these dimensions represent flat bipolar, "either-or" frameworks. As has been learned in the previous chapters, nothing is that simple when it comes to race. All of these dimensions are important components of the discussion: they carry at least a kernel of truth and therefore must be met with sincere appreciation. Racial issues have dogged this country since its birth. The complexities cannot be put in one box or seen through just one lens. Embracing, instead of explaining away, the paradoxes and apparent contradictions holds the key to progress.

The black-white paradigm, for example, is a necessary but an insufficient tool for understanding the current racial climate. In many ways, the story of the subjugation and the ensuing struggles of the African American population serves as the backdrop to the story of America itself. Even in the face of today's much-celebrated diversity, hate crime data show that black people continue to bear the cruelest brunt of social inequality, while other groups feel the sting and burn through discrimination, disproportionate poverty, and failing schools. The stubborn pull of the black-white axis prevents all racial and ethnic groups, including whites, from fully participating in this country's economic and social life.

The racial climate is changing. It is true that when talking about race, it is necessary to begin with an understanding of the experience of Native Americans. Further, an understanding of the past, continuing, and institutionalized racism that black people have endured is essential. But the experiences of different racial and ethnic groups need to be specifically analyzed and addressed. Culling through the journeys of Latinos, Native Americans, African Americans, and Asian Americans and examining their continuing challenges suggest that only thoughtful analysis that is informed by both history and present realities will yield effective strategies. While the differences among racial and ethnic groups need to be acknowledged, what the groups as a whole have in common is disproportionate poverty and discrimination that must be addressed.

The progress reflected by the growing acceptance of diversity in the United States—as well as impressive individual success stories among racial minorities—is not an illusion. It is true that the Latino community's political and cultural influence is expanding. It is true that blacks have made impressive strides in local politics, various professions, and the arts. And it is true that some Asian groups have made extraordinary educational and economic gains. However, it is a myth that simply welcoming diversity ushers in an era of social justice and racial harmony. Continuing and embedded prejudice prevents the vast majority of people of color from overcoming poverty, receiving fairness in the criminal justice system, attaining equal access to resources, and building political power. It would be premature to declare victory over racism and inequality.

These times call for solutions that reinforce universal goals and are tailored to the needs and concerns of particular groups. The differences between various racial and ethnic groups necessitate the latter. Similar problems manifest themselves in varied ways; there are multiple factors at play in any given situation. Poverty in the Latino community, for example, cannot be adequately addressed without an appreciation of how the experiences of Puerto Ricans diverge from those of Mexicans. Anti-Asian discrimination is very different from antiblack sentiment. These differences often demand targeted responses even though the universal goal of full participation is overriding. But as we have seen, strategies focused on one group sometimes yield dividends for all, as has been the case with the civil rights movement.

There is often an unnecessary disconnect between local efforts involved with addressing racial inequities and efforts that are national in scope. Local activists and policy makers have unique insight into their own communities' needs, and this wisdom should permeate state and national initiatives. Success on the local level, however, depends on the context set by the federal government. This is why we maintain that national policy must set the floor and the framework for achieving equity. Washington can either help or hinder local efforts to bridge racial divides; it cannot be neutral. As exemplified by the sprawl problem, the nation's urban and suburban areas must increasingly work in partnership to address interconnected issues.

Innovative approaches and solutions will emerge as this type of cooperative spirit takes root. The rethinking of suburban sprawl might result in a commitment to battle decay in urban neighborhoods. Interest in preserving the environment, a traditionally rural or suburban concern, might finally be translated into urban policy. The desire for global competitiveness could result in a sustained, productive focus on improving local school districts. In today's interdependent world, no one community can heal itself by itself. Effort by members of all communities will be necessary to achieve everyone's hopes and dreams.

Finally, it is time to abandon the old debates about the value of individual effort. Obviously, individual effort is required. The growth of minority small businesses demonstrates that people of color have the desire to succeed. However, individual success stories should not lead to complacency or pointing a finger of blame at those who remain behind. In low-income communities of color, the question is how to eradicate the structural barriers that impede the full expression of individual achievement and replace them with the tools that encourage wealth building.

Effective strategies to promote well-being and inclusion exist. The data presented in this book are intended to inform racial dialogue so that attempts at discourse are not hindered and derailed by arguments over what should be settled facts. What the country has lacked is the required public and political will to apply what is known at the scale needed to be fully effective. The future holds great promise. It will be hard to ignore demands from the growing minority populations. The advancements that are being made by all groups will continue to place more people with ties to Latino, Native American, Asian American, and African American groups in positions of influence, forcing attention on the issues of inclusion and full participation, but also allowing some very knowledgeable and committed people to begin to use their positions to directly address inequality.

The key will be leadership. Leaders of the future cannot sidestep painful discussions, and, ultimately, decisions. Race must be at the top of the agendas of all who seek to provide stewardship in the 21st century. The promise of America is within reach.

The way ahead is up to the American people—all of us.

Bibliography of Data Sources

To generate the figures, tables, and data analysis presented through *Searching for the Uncommon Common Ground*, we relied on two types of data sources: (a) broad based, universally acknowledged collections from which to extrapolate the "big picture" or overview of a given topic and (b) less widely known, but equally valid documentation from which to glean targeted, tailored details about a given situation or issue.

This bibliography of data sources is organized accordingly.

General

California Demographics
State of California, Department of Finance,
www.dof.ca.gov

Computer Access
National Telecommunications and Information Administration, www.ntia.doc.gov/;
www.digitaldivide.gov/reports.htm

Economic Status
U.S. Census Bureau, www.census.gov

Education
U.S. Census Bureau, www.census.gov
National Center for Education Statistics, nces.ed.gov/;
http://nces.ed.gov/naep3/tables/Ltt1999/

Health
U.S. Census Bureau, www.census.gov
National Center for Health Statistics,
www.cdc.gov/nchs/default.htm

Justice System
Federal Bureau of Investigation, www.fbi.gov

Labor Markets
Bureau of Labor Statistics, http://stats.bls.gov/
U.S. Census Bureau, www.census.gov

Polls and Surveys
The Gallup Organization–Princeton, www.gallup.com/

U.S. Demographics
Statistical Abstract of the United States 1999—CD ROM
Statistical Abstract of the United States 2000—Web version
U.S. Census Bureau, www.census.gov

U.S. Geographic Information Systems
U.S. Census Bureau, www.census.gov
ESRI GIS and Mapping Software, www.esri.com

Detailed Chart Sources

Chapter 1 Figures

1-1: *Statistical Abstract of the United States: The National Data Book*. Annual CD-ROM. Washington, DC: U.S. Department of Commerce. 1999. Section 1. Population. 2000 demographic estimates based on figures in

Table DP-1, Profiles of General Demographic Characteristics: 2000, in *Profiles of General Demographic Characteristics, 2000* (U.S. Census Bureau, May 2001).

1-2: *Statistical Abstract of the United States: The National Data Book*. Annual CD-ROM. Washington, DC: U.S. Department of Commerce. 1999. Section 1. Population.

1-3: State of California Department of Finance. Race/Ethnic Population with Age and Sex Detail, 1970–2040. Sacramento, CA, December 1998. <www.dof.ca.gov:8080/html/fs%5Fdata/stat%2Dabs/sec_B.htm>. 2000 estimates generated from the U.S. Census P.L. 94–171 Redistricting Data Summary File for California, using an algorithm to assign the mixed races numbers to distinct categories to maintain consistency with the 1990 calculations.

1-4: *Statistical Abstract of the United States: The National Data Book*. Annual CD-ROM. Washington, DC: U.S. Department of Commerce. 1999. Section 1. Population.

1-5: U.S. Census Bureau, Population Division, Population Projections Branch. "Projected State Populations, by Sex, Race, and Hispanic Origin: 1995–2025." Current Population Reports, July 5, 2001. <www.census.gov/population/projections/state/stpjrace.txt>.

Chapter 2 Figures

2-1: *The Hispanic Population, Census 2000 Brief*, U.S. Census Bureau, issued May 2001.

2-2: Table DP-1, Profiles of General Demographic Characteristics: 2000, in *Profiles of General Demographic Characteristics, 2000* (U.S. Census Bureau, May 2001).

2-3: Newport, Frank. "Americans Today Much More Accepting of a Woman, Black, Catholic, or Jew As President." The Gallup Organization-Princeton,

March 29, 1998. <www.gallup.com//poll/releases/pr990329.asp>.

2-4: Federal Bureau of Investigation. "Uniform Crime Reports." Hate Crime Statistics, Criminal Justice Information Services (CJIS) Division, May 4, 2001 <www.fbi.gov/ucr/ucr.htm>. The 1995 through the 1999 reports were used.

2-5: Ibid.

2-6: Massey, Douglas S., and Nancy A. Denton. *American Apartheid : Segregation and the Making of the Underclass*. Cambridge: Harvard University Press, 1993, p. 222.

2-7: Calculations from *The State of the Nation's Cities: A Comprehensive Database on American Cities and Suburbs*. Center for Urban Policy Research, Rutgers State University of New Jersey. <http://policy.rutgers.edu/cupr/indexlg.htm>. The SNC database, which includes information on seventy-four of the country's largest cities and metro areas, with most variables drawn from the 1970, 1980, and 1990 censuses, was compiled by Norman J. Glickman, Michael Lahr, and Elvin Wyly under HUD contract by the Center for Urban Policy Research to meet the data needs of the United Nations' Habitat II Conference held in Istanbul in June 1996 and has been expanded in variable coverage since. We specifically used version 2.11A (September 22, 1997).

Figure in Box 2-1: Calculated using the 1990 Public Use Microdata Sample; for details, see Pastor (2001).

Chapter 3 Figures

3-1: U.S. Census Bureau. "Race and Hispanic Origin of Householder-Families by Median and Mean Income: 1947 to 1999." Table F-5, March 1999 Current Population Survey, May 4, 2001. <www.census.gov/hhes/income/histinc/f05.html>.

3-2:   ———. "Race and Hispanic Origin of Householder-Households by Median and Mean Income: 1967 to 1999." Table H-5, March 1999 Current Population Survey, May 4, 2001 <www.census.gov/hhes/income/histinc/h05.html>.

3-3:   Bureau of Labor Statistics. "Employment Status of the Civilian Population by Race, Sex, Age, and Hispanic Origin." Table A-2, Labor Force Statistics, Current Population Survey, June 25, 2001. <http://stats.bls.gov/webapps/legacy/cpsatab2.htm>.

3-4:   ———. "Usual Weekly Earnings of Wage and Salary Workers." Archived News Releases, by quarter 1996–2001, June 25, 2001. <www.bls.gov/bls_news/archives/all_nr.htm#WKYENG>. Pre-1996 figures (adjusted to reflect the new base year for real calculations) taken from Executive Office of the President. "Median Usual Weekly Earnings of [Male/Female] Full-Time Workers." *Changing America—Indicators of Social and Economic Well-Being by Race and Hispanic Origin.* Washington, DC: Government Printing Office, 1998. <http://w3.access.gpo.gov/eop/ca/charts/index.html>.

3-5:   Ibid.

3-6:   U.S. Census Bureau, Poverty and Health Statistics Branch/HHES Division. "Poverty Status of People by Family Relationship, Race, and Hispanic Origin: 1959 to 1999." Table 2, Current Population Survey: 1959–1999, June 25, 2001. <www.census.gov/hhes/poverty/histpov/hstpov2.html>.

3-7:   ———. "Poverty Status of People, by Age, Race, and Hispanic Origin: 1959 to 1999." Table 3, Current Population Survey: 1959–1999, June 25, 2001. <www.census.gov/hhes/poverty/histpov/hstpov3.html>.

3-8:   ———. "Related Children in Female Householder Families as a Proportion of All Related Children, by

Poverty Status: 1959 to 1999." Table 10, Current Population Survey: 1959–1999, June 25, 2001. <www.census.gov/hhes/poverty/histpov/hstpov10.html>.

3-9: U.S. Census Bureau. "Living Arrangements of Black Children Under 18 Years Old: 1960 to Present." Table CH-3, Current Population Survey Reports, June 25, 2001. <www.census.gov/population/socdemo/ms-la/tabch-3.txt>.

3-10:———. "Children Without Health Insurance for the Entire Year by Age, Race, and Ethnicity: 1998 and 1999." Table 4, Current Population Survey, Health Insurance Coverage: 1999 (P60-211), June 25, 2001. <www.census.gov/hhes/hlthins/hlthin99/dtable4.html>.

3-11: National Center for Health Statistics. "Infant, neonatal, and postneonatal mortality rates, according to detailed race of mother and Hispanic origin of mother: United States, selected birth cohorts 1983–96." Table 19, Health United States 2000, with Adolescent Health Chartbook, June 25, 2001. <ftp://ftp.cdc.gov/pub/Health_Statistics/NCHS/Publications/Health_US/hus99/>.

3-12:———. "Life expectancy at birth, at 65 years of age, and at 75 years of age, according to race and sex: United States, selected years 1900–97." Health United States 2000, with Adolescent Health Chartbook. June 25, 2001. <ftp://ftp.cdc.gov/pub/Health_Statistics/NCHS/Publcations/Health_US/hus99/>.

3-13: Wolff, Edward N. "Recent Trends in Wealth Ownership, 1938–1998." *The Jerome Levy Economics Institute of Bard College*. April 2000, June 25, 2001. <www.levy.org/docs/wrkpap/papers/300.html>.

3-14: Ibid.

3-15: U.S. Census Bureau. "Gini Ratios for Families, by Race and Hispanic Origin of Householder: 1947 to 1999." Table F-4, March Current Population Survey,

March 5, 2001. <www.census.gov/hhes/income/histinc/f04.html>.

3-16: Calculated from *The State of the Nation's Cities* (SNC) (see Figure 2-7 source for more detailed reference).

3-17: Ibid.

3-18: Ibid.

Chapter 5 Figures

5-1: U.S. Census Bureau. "Percent of People 25 Years Old and Over Who Have Completed High School or College, by Race, Hispanic Origin, and Sex: Selected Years 1940 to 2000." Table A-2, March 2000 Current Population Survey, July 3, 2001 <www.census.gov/population/socdemo/education/tableA-2.txt>.

5-2: ———. "Mean Earnings of Workers 18 Years Old and Over, by Educational Attainment, Race, Hispanic Origin, and Sex: 1975 to 1999." Table A-3, March 2000 Current Population Survey, July 3, 2001. <www.census.gov/population/socdemo/education/tableA-3.txt>.

5-3: ———. "Enrollment Status of the Population 3 Years Old and Over, by Age, Gender, Race, Hispanic Origin, Nativity, and Selected Educational Characteristics: October 1998." Table 1, October 1998 Current Population Survey, July 3, 2001. <www.census.gov/population/socdemo/school/report98/tab01.txt>.

5-4: National Center for Education Statistics. "NAEP 1999 Long-Term Trend Reading Summary Data Tables for Age 9 Student Data." National Assessment of Educational Progress, The Nation's Report Card, July 3, 2001.<http://nces.ed.gov/nationsreportcard/tables/Ltt 1999/NTR11012.asp>. From the same source, "NAEP 1999 Long-Term Trend Reading Summary Data Tables for Age 13 Student Data" and "NAEP 1999 Long-Term Trend Reading Summary Data Tables for Age 17 Student Data."

5-5: Gallup Organization–Princeton. "Gallup Poll Social Audit on Black/White Relations in the U.S., conducted from September 24–November 16, 1999." Poll Topics Race Relations, July 3, 2001. <www.gallup.com/poll/indicators/indrace.asp>.

5-6: Ibid.

5-7: Morello-Frosch, Rachel, Manuel Pastor, and James Sadd. "Environmental Justice and Southern California's 'Riskscape': The Distribution of Air Toxics Exposures and Health Risks Among Diverse Communities." *Urban Affairs Review,* 36.4 (2001): 551–578.

5-8: Calculated from data in three reports from the National Telecommunications and Information Administration: *Falling Through the Net: Toward Digital Inclusion* (2000), *Falling Through the Net: Defining the Digital Divide* (1999), and *Falling Through the Net II: New Data on the Digital Divide* (1998), specifically Chart 12 from the 1998 report, Chart A-10 from the 1999 report, and Figure I-13 from the 2000 report. All reports can be obtained at <www.ntia.doc.gov/ntia home/digitaldivide>.

5-9: Calculated from data in three reports from the National Telecommunications and Information Administration: *Falling Through the Net: Toward Digital Inclusion* (2000), *Falling Through the Net: Defining the Digital Divide* (1999), and *Falling Through the Net II: New Data on the Digital Divide* (1998), specifically Chart 21 from the 1998 report, Chart I-23 from the 1999 report, and Figure I-10 from the 2000 report. All reports can be obtained at <www.ntia.doc.gov/ntia home/digitaldivide>.

5-10: National Telecommunications and Information Administration. Calculated from data in *Falling Through the Net: Toward Digital Inclusion,* October 2000, specifically Figures A5 and A11. <www.ntia.doc.gov/

ntiahome/fttn00/charts00.html#a96>and<www.ntia. doc.gov/ntiahome/fttn00/charts00.html#a99>.

5-11: U.S. Census Bureau, Population Division, Campbell Gibson and Emily Lennon. "Historical Census Statistics on the Foreign-born Population of the United States: 1850–1990." Population Division Working Papers 29. July 3, 2001. <www.census.gov/population/ www/documentation/twps0029/twps0029.html>.

5-12: Ibid.

5-13: U.S. Bureau of Justice Statistics. "Estimated Number and Percent of Adults under Correctional Supervision by Sex and Race, United States, 1985–1997." Table 6.2, *The Sourcebook of Criminal Justice Statistics, 1999*, July 3, 2001. <www.albany.edu/sourcebook/1995/tost_6 .html>.

5-14: Gallup Organization–Princeton. "Gallup Poll Social Audit on Black/White Relations in the U.S., conducted from September 24–November 16, 1999." Poll Topics Race Relations, July 3, 2001. <www.gallup.com/ poll/indicators/indrace.asp>.

Figure for Box 5-3: Data from *The Hispanic Population, Census 2000 Brief*, U.S. Census Bureau, issued May 2001.

Final Report
of the
Ninety-Eighth
American Assembly

At the close of their discussions, the participants in the Ninety-eighth American Assembly, on "Racial Equality: Public Policies for the Twenty-first Century," at Arden House, Harriman, New York, April 19–22, 2001, reviewed as a group the following statement. This statement represents general agreement; however, no one was asked to sign it. Furthermore, it should be understood that not everyone agreed with all of it.

Preamble

By the middle of this century, the United States will no longer be a majority non-Hispanic white nation—and the very concept and meaning of race will have evolved. The early results from the 2000 census indicate that our diversity has already increased dramatically, even within minority communities. The Latino population now equals that of African Americans; the Asian American and Pacific Islander population is on a rapid ascent; and nearly 7 million Americans checked more than one racial box in the census that first allowed this possibility.

Founded in 1950, shortly before the Supreme Court ushered in a new era promising racial justice in its landmark *Brown v. Board of Education* decision, The American Assembly has played an important role in addressing major public policy topics. Today, almost a half-century later, the clarion call of *Brown* remains as relevant to racial equality as it was then. Indeed, the profound problems of racial discrimination and segregation as well as the tremendous potential of remedies have become even more important over time. Accordingly, this American Assembly takes up racial equality with an appropriate seriousness of purpose and renewed commitment to achieving social justice.

Race is arguably the most difficult issue for people to discuss. As our group, representing racial, ideological, and geographical differences, met at Arden House on the future of racial equality in the United States, there was significant discussion and debate. Our personal experiences—of success and frustration, of bridge building and distrust—influence views on race and public policy in a way not always present in other arenas. Moreover, we may be unconscious of our racial assumptions, and institutionally and structurally caused racial disparities can arise and persist even though individuals are well-meaning. Our search for consensus was never easy and not always successful. Still, we looked not for the lowest common denominator, but rather for the most challenging level of agreement—"the uncommon common ground."

We found this in several different arenas. First, we called for a new kind of leadership and political courage. Leaders and followers often find it difficult to move beyond individual perceptions and short-term interests to lift up common values and invest in a shared moral and political framework. We therefore need leadership that seeks not to scapegoat others or isolate itself, but rather, brings us together, seeing beyond the zero sum frameworks to the win-win possibilities. In this regard, the participation of young leaders who came from across the United States, with their commitment to community building, was insightful and inspirational.

Second, there is an urgent need for communication and action at every level. Our meeting on racial equality followed several days of civil unrest in Cincinnati, triggered by the police shooting of an unarmed black youth. This was reminiscent of other shootings and came at a time when exposure of patterns of racial profiling has undermined community-police relations. While there has been important progress in areas such as racial attitudes and anti-segregation laws, many participants warned that the gap between our country's seeming acceptance of our new diversity and our simultaneous failure to decrease disparities in economic, educational, and social outcomes spells trouble for our shared future. Others noted the needs of the economy and business, and suggested that it was foolish to abandon growing markets in low-income neighborhoods, fail to contract with strong minority business, or abandon large portions of the emerging workforce.

Thus, it is necessary to revisit our basic assumptions as the decisions we make in the next five years will set the course on race relations for the next twenty-five years. Nonetheless, even as we lay out a vision for the future, we stress that if we do not act now, generations of youth will be under-prepared, our capacity to thrive in the global economy will suffer, and our democratic values and practices will be eroded.

Finally, broad based change is necessary. We were guided by the courage and commitment of participants of color, as well as by the courage and commitment of the white participants, who have challenged the structures of racism. We were inspired by one participant's account of her efforts to help two teenage boys in difficult circumstances to stay in school and succeed. But while we celebrate and honor these efforts to change our country one life at a time, we also recognize that achieving a world in which *all* of us can maximize our potential will require new vision, new lan-

guage, new strategies, new leadership, and much more vig-
orous action in both public and private sectors.

A Vision for 2025

Our vision for 2025 is simple: giving new life to the promise
of equality and the enduring, but unfulfilled, ideal of liberty
and justice for all. Achieving this vision will require effort by
all, including the exercise of both societal and individual
responsibility, a desire to move beyond tolerance of difference
to valuing diversity, and a willingness to work for a common
good in which everyone has real opportunity and can participate in a fair process. We firmly believe that opportunity and
outcomes are interrelated and that measuring results is key to
testing whether opportunity is being achieved.

In our path forward, we are guided by the values of
interconnectedness, commitment, democracy, and dignity.
By interconnectedness, we mean a full recognition of the
web of human relations, the common values that connect
us all, and our connection to the earth itself. By commitment, we mean a recognition by people of all races and ethnicities that it is not in their interest to have a society where
race and ethnicity dictate one's economic and social outcomes. By democracy, we mean ensuring the voice and
power of people of different economic, social, political,
racial, and ethnic backgrounds in the public decision-
making process. By dignity, we mean a new social contract
that includes high standards—such as living wages and fair
working conditions, access to healthcare and quality education—so that individuals can fully participate in and contribute to our society with an improved quality of life.

To achieve these goals, stakeholders need to be able to
talk openly and honestly about color, class, culture, and
privilege. While some worry about the "fatigue" that could
result from rehashing history, we need to face up to a past
of discrimination and injustice, moving forward, while
acknowledging the need for reconciliation. The genocidal

assault on Native Americans and their treatment as less than human set the stage for racism in the United States and the mistreatment of all people of color. Moreover, the black-white experience of slavery and Jim Crow has been central and defining for our society. We need to acknowledge that these wounds have yet to heal, even as we open our minds to the realities of new immigrants, their concerns and needs, and the changing meanings of race.

Reaching for Social and Economic Justice

Though race and ethnicity have some impact on virtually every aspect of life in the United States, the constraints of time led us to focus on a few specific areas of policy and politics. While the list of issues discussed is by no means exhaustive, they illustrate the kinds of racial challenges that Americans will increasingly face. We believe they illuminate some of the broader, more philosophical choices that arise in the course of considering many other questions of racial and ethnic inequality.

In four days of wide-ranging conversation, we touched on questions of economics, education, healthcare, housing, affirmative action, among others. Nevertheless, the agenda for this Assembly focused on areas where our dialogue could lead to significant progress: criminal justice, immigration, and economic opportunity. We believe that both the nation and democracy as we know it will be severely threatened if we as a country do not come together to move forward on these matters.

One larger philosophical question that we considered in our deliberations was the appropriate mix of "universal" and "particular" strategies. Universal solutions can be effective in addressing the class based component of the challenges facing many minority communities, and it is often easier to garner political support for proposals that are cast in race-neutral language. For example, raising the minimum wage, increasing the Earned Income Tax Credit, enacting legislation for universal health insurance, teaching all children a second language, and ensuring that every teenager graduates from high school with a meaningful diploma are policies that would have significant benefits for all of us, especially for people of color. Yet, many of the problems experienced by people of color are specific to their communities. Such problems, whether rooted in history or the consequence of continuing discrimination, can best be addressed by particular, targeted solutions, including affirmative action and programs designed to help minorities and immigrants participate fully in society.

However, in dealing with real-world problems, most participants believe this to be a false dichotomy. In many cases, the goal will be universal, but the particular strategies applied in any given instance may have to be tailored to the community at hand. For example, a campaign designed to insure that every teen finishes high school will of necessity take a different form in a poor, largely Vietnamese-speaking, urban neighborhood than in an under-populated, predominantly white, rural region. While a distinct minority of participants felt that universal approaches were generally to be preferred, we overwhelmingly felt that racial inequality should be analyzed instance-by-instance, as well as in terms of its societal impact to determine the appropriate policy remedy or political strategy, taking into consideration the particular circumstances of people of color and the extensiveness and tenacity of privilege.

Criminal Justice

There is significant racial disparity in most aspects of law enforcement, including disparate treatment by police, selective prosecution, and discriminatory sentencing. The prominence of these issues and the high profile incidents that capture the attention of the public represent a crisis, which erodes the willingness of people of color to trust the system and reinforces a sense that social justice is lacking in a nation that celebrates its commitment to freedom and democracy.

The evidence of the current crisis is all around us. Two million individuals are incarcerated in America, and over two-thirds of them are people of color. The "war on drugs"—responsible for a significant share of this incarceration—has failed our communities and has contributed to a loss of confidence in the criminal justice system. Even though actual crime rates have decreased, media coverage fosters negative racial stereotypes and distrust across racial lines. Racial profiling creates a siege mentality within communities of color. The death penalty is disproportionately applied to people of color and those in the lowest socioeconomic strata. People of color are far more likely to be arrested and, once in custody, to have their rights violated. Once convicted of a crime, disparate penalties and mandatory sentences destroy families and create a sense of hopelessness in our communities. While in prison, nonviolent offenders face a penal system that often results in further criminalization as opposed to rehabilitation.

Our vision of racial justice requires a judicial system in which all laws are fairly and equitably enforced, every community feels protected and not victimized, sentencing is accepted as fair, and there is investment and belief in rehabilitation. In our vision, communities and law enforcement are partners in community building, which includes reaching out to our youth, creating innovative crime prevention strategies, building more positive relations between police officers and community residents, and community evaluation of policing. These will both reduce the demands on our criminal justice system and improve the quality of life in our neighborhoods.

To remedy these problems, we need to take steps both large and small:

• We should end the practice of trying juveniles as adults, as well as end the practice of placing juvenile and adult offenders in the same facilities. We should also cease incarcerating nonviolent with violent offenders, especially youth.

- We should call a halt to the flawed "war on drugs" and recognize that education, prevention, and treatment must become more prominent elements of our efforts to combat the corrosive effects of drug abuse.
- Mandatory minimum sentences, and their accompanying contribution to the exponential growth of prisons, should be abolished, as should disparities in sentencing, e.g., for crack versus powdered cocaine offenses.
- Racial profiling in all its forms and manifestations is a discriminatory practice. It reinforces negative stereotypes and further undermines the relationship between the police and the community. It must end immediately.
- We should provide competent and fairly compensated indigent defense.
- We should renew an emphasis on effective rehabilitation and restore the voting rights of those who have paid their debt to society, supporting their return as participating members of our democracy.

Immigration

Our population today has a higher proportion of foreign-born people than it has had in decades, and immigrants live in every state and almost every community. These increased numbers have challenged our understanding of fairness and inclusion, especially with the predominantly non-European makeup of today's immigrant population.

Immigration is good for the country, but has not been good for all immigrants. Immigrants should be entitled to the full rights of life, liberty, and the pursuit of happiness, and be provided with the same opportunities and protections as all Americans to develop to their full potential.

To achieve the goal of racial justice, we must look at how our country develops immigration policy and treats its immigrants. The black-white paradigm forged out of the legacy of slavery, segregation, and discrimination—conditions that need increased attention and remedies—is not broad enough to explain the unique experiences of nonblack immigrant groups. For example, Asian Americans and Latinos, among others, can be discriminated against based on language or perceived foreign appearance. In addition, immigrants of non-European heritage are often not considered "real" Americans. Even Asian Americans and Latinos with a multigenerational history in the United States encounter discriminatory treatment because of their heritage. Thinking more broadly about race should not diminish the importance of the black-white dynamic, but it should help us to understand others' experiences with discrimination.

We must recognize the effect of globalization that leads to the migration of peoples across national boundaries, and this calls for the examination of global solutions. But in terms of U.S. policy, we recommend the following:

- We need to ensure that immigration policies are inclusive and fair. Immigrants must be entitled to full due process in deportation proceedings; we find current law, which allows evidence to be concealed from immigrants and their counsel during deportation hearings, to be particularly objectionable and contrary to our values of justice.
- The Immigration and Naturalization Service should rebalance its contradictory functions of enforcing immigration laws and providing services, with a heavier emphasis on the task of incorporating new immigrants into American society.
- Other institutions could also play an important role. For example, the AFL-CIO recently reversed its long-held policy against increased immigration and now embraces immigrant workers and advocates for their full employment rights and protections, and for legalization of undocumented workers.
- Immigrants must feel at full liberty to report violations of their rights. Immigrants, with or without work authorization, must be protected from employer reprisals when they assert their workplace rights such

as wage and safety laws, anti-discrimination laws, and the right to organize.

- We recommend that The American Assembly develop another program on immigration to address the complexity of immigration and immigrant policies with an emphasis on racial justice.

Economic Opportunity

The correlation between race and income inequity remains strong, and a variety of concerns were raised as a part of a larger conversation about economic justice. Racial disparities can and should be reduced through short-term strategies such as raising the minimum wage, increasing the Earned Income Tax Credit, and protecting the self-organization of workers, policies that will help all disadvantaged groups. We should also use our power as consumers to support businesses of all sizes—wherever located—that have the following characteristics: outstanding records of hiring, training, and promoting women and people of color; investment in low-income communities; active contracting with businesses owned by people of color; and a practice of training minority professionals to assume larger and more significant roles in the United States economy. We urge the design and implementation of a national purchasing campaign to support businesses that aggressively address the many issues and national problems that negatively impact race relations in our country.

In addition, longer-term strategies should be developed to ensure that people of color are key contributors and recipients of the economic gains. This will include tackling complex issues, such as education reform, suburban sprawl and urban reinvestment, and the digital economy.

Education Reform. Quality public education is key to reducing inequalities of both outcomes and opportunities. At the same time, the education gap between whites and disadvantaged groups, as measured by academic achievement and the quality of instruction and facilities, is only increasing. A successful public education system is critical to the future of our democracy and must be one of our highest priorities. The public education system, complemented by private initiatives on the part of businesses, faith based institutions, foundations, and child- and youth-development organizations, must assure that every child receives personal attention from competent, caring adults to enable him or her to reach full potential academically and personally. Support from younger people is similarly important. These issues are not just academic but also involve attention to athletic, artistic, and vocational interests that are critical to the motivation of each unique individual.

As a nation, we need to commit to do the following:

- Reform an education system that is embattled, still segregated, and is often no longer viewed as a well-functioning public institution.
- Develop a curriculum that actively includes and welcomes traditionally silenced voices, addresses historic and current racial injustice, and focuses on fostering critical thinking in youth.
- Aggressively invest in K–12 education by all approaches that are consistent with basic constitutional principles and are inextricably linked with qualitative and quantitative outcomes.
- Demand that the government be committed to restructuring public school financing by changing from the current property tax–dominated system for public schools toward a more stable funding base that provides sufficient resources for economically disadvantaged communities.
- Affirm education in the broader context of community building by understanding education as critical in creating an active and engaged public. As part of this effort, we must create a sense of community in schools, so that students, parents, and teachers as well as civic

and corporate leaders are all a part of the conversation and participate in a shared response.

Suburban Sprawl & Urban Reinvestment. We must question patterns of metropolitan development that perpetuate segregation and divide groups from each other. Suburban sprawl has been subsidized by the public sector through mechanisms like highway construction, sewage treatment, and mortgage interest deduction. These patterns of development almost always assure the destruction of the natural environment and its ecosystems, as well as erode a sense of community and the accompanying commitment to shared purpose and responsibility. Metropolitan regions must be willing to undertake the difficult tasks of increasing linkages between cities and suburbs and building relationships and understanding across racial, class, and geographic boundaries. To do this, concrete measures must be undertaken to reduce patterns of racial discrimination and racial isolation, such as creating affordable housing throughout the region close to employment, increasing incentives for investment in urban areas, and promoting equitable development in neighborhoods where people of color reside that reduces displacement and provides opportunities for ownership by residents of homes and businesses.

Digital Economy. Employment opportunities and promotion to higher paying jobs are increasingly dependent on familiarity with digital technology. It is therefore incumbent on all schools and libraries, and nonprofit organizations and businesses, to have the funding and leadership to provide access to and training in these technologies, and to recognize that these technologies are essential for the social and economic development of all people, including those of color.

Leadership and Political Courage

To achieve the goals in this report, including addressing successfully the racial and ethnic divisions that threaten our democracy and engaging the public with the challenges of racial justice and equality, we need leaders who combine a wide range of qualities. Among the most important are an ability to lead communities in developing a shared vision of racial justice and equality and implementing an action plan that achieves that vision. These leaders must also:

- Reflect the diversity of our changing demographics.
- Have the capacity to deal with ever more complex issues in an integrated and collaborative fashion and have the ability to work across racial and ethnic groups, and with leaders from public, private, and nonprofit sectors.
- Rise above short-term individual interests to invest in a shared moral framework for the long-term good of the entire community.
- Seek to build bridges within and across all communities, rather than promoting intolerance and polarization.

Once identified, the public should hold these leaders accountable to this long-term collective good.

We must also focus on identifying and building the capacity of current leaders, while at the same time creating and supporting programs that build a new generation of leadership. We therefore suggest the following:

- Foundations and other institutions should collaborate to make investment in leadership development a top priority, ranging from programs that begin in elementary schools to those that foster multicultural and multisector collaboration among current leaders.
- A commitment to exploring innovative ways of teaching civics is an important building block to develop youth leadership. This new direction should begin in elementary schools with a new civics curriculum that encompasses multicultural realities and histories of shared struggles, conflict mediation, democracy, and

strategies for positive change. It should also include mentoring and service opportunities that cut across racial, ethnic, and class lines.

- Corporations should work to achieve a more responsible and diverse leadership within the private sector and invest in building the leadership capacities of the communities that their businesses affect.

Media leaders have a particularly critical role to play in impeding or advancing the ability of communities to build sufficient public understanding and commitment to facing the difficult issues of racial justice and equality. While media at times play a powerful role in forging a consensus in support of social progress and tough choices, all too often media superficially and inaccurately frame race issues because of their focus on conflict and sensationalism. More media leaders must therefore become multiculturally literate and racially and ethnically representative, and ensure that they are providing increasingly comprehensive, balanced, and accurate coverage and programming.

A Call to Action

Awareness of and commitment to address the racial and ethnic disparities in this country have declined. Increasing global interconnectedness, and rapidly changing demographics, are assets; however, pernicious stereotyping and persistent inequalities have weakened our social fabric and threaten to undermine the health of our democracy. Whole segments of our society have little or no voice in influencing our institutions and shaping our collective destiny. It is imperative that we as a country reframe how we address issues of race and ethnicity and develop a consensus on a social contract around the principles of racial justice and equality.

We therefore call on leaders from every sector and community in our society to:

- Develop a shared new vision of racial justice;
- Build multiracial and multiethnic coalitions;
- Commit to a plan of action that incorporates the recommendations in this report and moves this country towards a new vision of uniting America.

Participants
The Ninety-Eighth American Assembly

† ABDULWAHAB
  ALKEBSI
Deputy Director
American Muslim Council
Washington, DC

† JOE ALVAREZ
Regional Director
AFL-CIO, Northeast Region
New York, NY

★ ANGELA GLOVER
  BLACKWELL
Founder and President
PolicyLink
Oakland, CA

■ HON. J. KENNETH
  BLACKWELL
Secretary of State
State of Ohio
Columbus, OH

MARIA BLANCO MALDEF
National Senior Counsel
Sacramento, CA

MARIA BUSTRIA
Harriman Fellow
Columbia University
New York, NY

JOSE CALDERON
*Professor of Sociology and
  Chicano Studies*
Pitzer College
Claremont, CA

REV. JOAN BROWN
  CAMPBELL
Director of Religion
Chautauqua Institution
Chautauqua, NY

DEBRA CARR
Chair, Interagency Task Force
UN World Conference
  Against Racism, Racial
  Discrimination,
  Xenophobia and Related
  Intolerance
Washington, DC

ELIZABETH PHILLIPS
COLLINS
Senior Program Leader
Florida Sheriffs Youth
Ranches, Inc.
Barberville, FL

• LEE CULLUM
Columnist
Dallas Morning News
Dallas, TX

DAYNA CUNNINGHAM
Associate Director
Rockefeller Foundation
New York, NY

BRADLEY CURREY, JR.
Retired Chairman & CEO
Rock-Tenn Company
Atlanta, GA

SHELDON DANZIGER
*Professor of Social Work and
Public Policy*
University of Michigan
Ann Arbor, MI

VERÓNICA DE LA CRUZ
Attorney/Alumna
Fulfillment Fund
Los Angeles, CA

JASON ELLIOTT
Managing Partner
Ranger Capital
Woody Creek, CO

ROBERT M. ENTMAN
Professor and Head
Department of
Communication
North Carolina State
University
Raleigh, NC

LEO ESTRADA
Associate Professor
UCLA, School of Public
Policy and Social
Research
Los Angeles, CA

* MARSHA JOHNSON
EVANS
National Executive Director
Girl Scouts of the USA
New York, NY

KENDRA FIELD
Harriman Fellow
Harvard University
Cambridge, MA

REV. C. WELTON GADDY
Executive Director
The Interfaith Alliance
Foundation
Washington, DC

** CHRIS GATES
President
National Civic League
Denver, CO

* JAMES GIBSON
Senior Fellow
The Center for the Study of
  Social Policy
Washington, DC

HON. VANESSA D.
  GILMORE
United States District Judge
U.S. District Court, South-
  ern District of Texas
Houston, TX

† RICHARD A. GROUNDS
Euchee Language Project
University of Tulsa
Tulsa, OK

■ LANI GUINIER
Professor
Harvard Law School
Cambridge, MA

REBECCA HAMLIN
Coordinator
Multicultural Youth Project
Chicago, IL

VICKIE HARRIS
Director, Corporate Diversity
Hallmark Cards, Inc.
Kansas City, MO

CLAIRE HATAMIYA
Senior Trainer
Global Kids
New York, NY

JOE HICKS
Executive Director
Human Relations Commis-
  sion, City of Los Angeles
Los Angeles, CA

BENI IVEY
Executive Director
Center for Democratic
  Renewal
Atlanta, GA

JUAN D. JOHNSON
*Vice President and Director of
  Diversity Strategies*
The Coca-Cola Company
Atlanta, GA

ELAINE JONES
President and Director Counsel
NAACP Legal Defense and
  Educational Fund, Inc.
New York, NY

BONGHWAN KIM
Executive Director
The Multicultural
  Collaborative
Los Angeles, CA

MICHELLE KOREJKO
Assistant Manager
Greater Philadelphia High
  School Partnership
Philadelphia, PA

★ STEWART KWOH
President and Executive Director
Asian Pacific American
  Legal Center of South-
  ern California
Los Angeles, CA

JAMES H. LOWRY
Vice President
Boston Consulting Group
Chicago, IL

ANTOINETTE
  MALVEAUX
President and CEO
The National Black MBA
  Association, Inc.
Chicago, IL

PHILLIP L. MARTIN
Race Relations Correspondent
National Public Radio
Washington, DC

JUAN D. MARTÍNEZ
Attorney-at-Law
"I Have A Dream" Founda-
  tion
New York, NY

JIMMY McGEE, III
*Associate Director, Multi Eth-
  nic Ministries*
Intervarsity Christian
  Fellowship
Atlanta, GA

DONALD F. McHENRY
*Distinguished Professor
  of Diplomacy*
School of Foreign Service
Georgetown University
Washington, DC

MICHAEL MEYERS
Executive Director
New York Civil Rights
  Coalition
New York, NY

KISCHA KAI MILLER
Planning and Policy Analyst
The Educational Alliance,
  Inc.
New York, NY

* KAREN K. NARASAKI
Executive Director
National Asian Pacific
  American Legal
  Consortium
Washington, DC

MONICA L. NEWMAN
*Vice President, Corporate
  Affairs*
Bank of America
Charlotte, NC

† ROSE OCHI
Monterey Park, CA

MELVIN L. OLIVER
*Vice President, Asset Building
  & Community Development
  Program*
The Ford Foundation
New York, NY

★ MANUEL PASTOR, JR.
Professor, Latin American and
Latino Studies
Director, Center for Justice,
Tolerance, and Community
University of California,
Santa Cruz
Santa Cruz, CA

DEVAL L. PATRICK
Executive Vice President and
General Counsel
The Coca-Cola Company
Atlanta, GA

ROBERT PHILLIPS
Associate
PolicyLink
Oakland, CA

† JOHN A. POWELL
Executive Director/Professor
of Law
Institute on Race and
Poverty
University of Minnesota
Minneapolis, MN

GERALD REYNOLDS
Senior Regulatory Attorney
Kansas City Power and
Light Company
Kansas City, MO

PAUL SCHMITZ
President and CEO
Public Allies
Milwaukee, WI

** JAI SOOKPRASERT
Senior Governmental Relations
Representative
California School
Employees Association
Sacramento, CA

EDSON W. SPENCER
Former Chair, Ford
Foundation
Retired CEO, Honeywell,
Inc.
Spencer Associates
Minneapolis, MN

MAUREEN S.
STEINBRUNER
President
Center for National Policy
Washington, DC

INÉS TALAMANTEZ
Associate Professor
Native American Religions,
Philosophies and
Chicano Studies
University of California,
Santa Barbara
Santa Barbara, CA

REV. W. DOUGLAS
TANNER, JR.
President
The Faith and Politics
Institute
Washington, DC

VERONICA TERRIQUEZ
Site Coordinator
Youth Together Project
Oakland, CA

DR. MELANIE
   TERVALON
Assistant Clinical Professor
University of California,
   San Francisco
San Francisco, CA

JAIME E. UZETA
*Director, Strategic Partnerships
   & Public Affairs*

MTV
New York, NY

** ARTURO VARGAS
Executive Director
National Association of
   Latino Elected &
   Appointed Officials, Inc.
   (NALEO) Educational
   Fund
Los Angeles, CA

LORI VILLAROSA
Program Officer
C.S. Mott Foundation
Flint, MI

FRANK H. WU
Associate Professor
Howard University Law
   School
Washington, DC

LINYEE S. YUAN
Harriman Fellow
Columbia University
New York, NY

★ Co-Director
* Discussion Leader
**Rapporteur

■ Speaker
• Moderator
† Panelist

Uniting America
Leadership Advisory Group
(in formation)

Co-Chairs

David R. Gergen

JFK School of Government, Harvard; *The NewsHour with Jim Lehrer*

Karen Elliott House

President, International, Dow Jones & Company, Inc.; *Wall Street Journal*

Donald F. McHenry

Georgetown University; Former U.S. Ambassador to the UN

Paul H. O'Neill

(on leave for government service as Secretary of Treasury) Former Chairman, ALCOA

Members

Paul A. Allaire

Chairman, Xerox Corporation

Jonathan Alter

Senior Editor, *Newsweek*

Derek Bok

Former President, Harvard University

David L. Boren

President, University of Oklahoma

Michael J. Boskin

Tully M. Friedman Professor of Economics, Hoover Institution, Stanford University

Bill Bradley	Former United States Senator (New Jersey)
Joan Brown Campbell	Director of Religion, Chautauqua Institution; Former General Secretary, National Council of Churches of Christ
Henry G. Cisneros	Chairman & CEO, American CityVista
John F. Cooke	Executive Vice President for External Affairs, The J. Paul Getty Trust
Lee Cullum	Columnist, *Dallas Morning News*
Mario Cuomo	Former Governor of New York
Douglas N. Daft	Chairman & CEO, The Coca-Cola Company
Thomas R. Donahue	AFL-CIO (Independent)
Peggy Dulany	Chair, The Synergos Institute
Don Eberly	(on leave for government service as Deputy Director and Deputy Assistant to the President/Office of Faith-Based and Community Initiatives) Former Chair & CEO, National Fatherhood Initiative; Director, Civil Society Project
Marian Wright Edelman	President, The Children's Defense Fund
Jeffrey A. Eisenach	President, Progress and Freedom Foundation
Marsha Johnson Evans	Rear Adm., U.S. Navy (Ret'd); National Executive Director, Girl Scouts of the USA
Dianne Feinstein	United States Senator (California)
Jim Florio	Former Governor of New Jersey

Robert M. Franklin	President, Interdenominational Theological Center
David P. Gardner	President Emeritus of the University of California and University of Utah
John W. Gardner	Consulting Professor, Graduate School of Education, Stanford University
William George	Chairman & CEO, Medtronic
Peter C. Goldmark, Jr.	CEO, *International Herald Tribune*
Michael Goodwin	President, Office and Professional Employees - International Union
William H. Gray III	President and CEO, United Negro College Fund, Inc.
David E. Hayes-Bautista	Director of UCLA Center for the Study of Latino Health & Culture and Professor of Medicine, School of Medicine, UCLA
Bryan J. Hehir	Chair of the Executive Committee, Professor of the Practice in Religion and Society, Harvard Divinity School, Harvard University
Antonia Hernandez	President and General Counsel, MALDEF
Irvine O. Hockaday, Jr.	President and CEO, Hallmark Cards, Inc.
Alice S. Huang	Senior Counselor for External Relations, California Institute of Technology
Charlayne Hunter-Gault	National Correspondent, *The NewsHour with Jim Lehrer*
Frank Keating	Governor of Oklahoma
Robert D. Kennedy	Retired Chairman, Union Carbide Corporation

William D. Ruckelshaus	Chairman and CEO, Browning Ferris Industries
George Rupp	President, Columbia University
Henry B. Schacht	Chairman and CEO, Lucent Technologies Inc.
Arthur Schlesinger, Jr.	Department of History, City University of New York; Author and Historian
Adele Simmons	Vice Chair, Chicago Metropolis 2020
Alan K. Simpson	Director, Institute of Politics, Harvard University
Edward Skloot	Executive Director, Surdna Foundation, Inc.
Edson W. Spencer	Former CEO, Honeywell Inc.; Former Chair, Ford Foundation
Chang-Lin Tien	Former Chancellor, UC Berkeley; Chairman, The Asia Foundation
Vin Weber	Former United States Congressman (Minnesota)
Frank A. Weil	Chairman, Abacus & Associates, Inc.
John C. Whitehead	Former Deputy Secretary of State; Former Chair, AEA Investors Inc.
William Julius Wilson	Professor, John F. Kennedy School of Government, Harvard University
Michael Woo	Director, Los Angeles Programs, L.I.S.C.
Daniel Yankelovich	President, Public Agenda Foundation
Alice Young	Chair, Asia Pacific Practice (U.S.), Kaye, Scholer, Fierman, Hays & Handler

About The American Assembly

The American Assembly was established by Dwight D. Eisenhower at Columbia University in 1950. It holds nonpartisan meetings and publishes authoritative books to illuminate issues of United States policy.

An affiliate of Columbia, the Assembly is a national, educational institution incorporated in the state of New York.

The Assembly seeks to provide information, stimulate discussion, and evoke independent conclusions on matters of vital public interest.

American Assembly Sessions

At least two national programs are initiated each year. Authorities are retained to write background papers presenting essential data and defining the main issues of each subject.

A group of men and women representing a broad range of experience, competence, and American leadership meet for several days to discuss the Assembly topic and consider alternatives for national policy.

All Assemblies follow the same procedure. The background papers are sent to participants in advance of the Assembly. The Assembly meets in small groups for four lengthy periods. All groups use the same agenda. At the close of these informal sessions participants adopt in plenary session a final report of findings and recommendations.

Regional, state, and local Assemblies are held following the national session at Arden House. Assemblies have also been held in England, Switzerland, Malaysia, Canada, the Caribbean, South America, Central America, the Philippines, China, and Taiwan. Over 160 institutions have cosponsored one or more Assemblies.

Arden House

The home of The American Assembly and the scene of the national sessions is Arden House, which was given to Columbia University in 1950 by W. Averell Harriman. E. Roland Harriman joined his brother in contributing toward adaptation of the property for conference purposes. The buildings and surrounding land, known as the Harriman Campus of Columbia University, are fifty miles north of New York City.

Arden House is a distinguished conference center. It is self-supporting and operates throughout the year for use by organizations with educational objectives. The American Assembly is a tenant of this Columbia University facility only during Assembly sessions.

Index